Beyond the House Plant

Beyond the House Plant

by JACK KRAMER

*How to create a garden
from your thriving house plants
in—and out of—doors*

Ballantine Books, New York

Library of Congress Catalog Card Number: 75-44369
ISBN 0-345-24876-7-395

Manufactured in the United States of America
First Edition: March, 1976

Acknowledgments

I wish to express my thanks to the following people who allowed us to photograph their indoor and outdoor no-land gardens:

Varney Boyl
Randal C. Oyler
Ray Mishler
Lehrs Greenhouse Restaurant
Dan DeGunthen
Andrew R. Addkison

And a special thanks again to my artist, Michael Valdez, who did the beautiful scratchboard drawings, and another vote of gratitude to Judy Smith, who typed and retyped my words.

Jack Kramer

Drawing Credits

Chapter 2:
Planter Boxes (Michael Valdez)

Chapter 3:
Planter Box Garden (Dean Snyder)
Shelf Garden (Dean Snyder)
Pyramid Window Greenhouse (Dean Snyder)
Pyramid Window Greenhouse (detail) (Dean Snyder)
Removing a Window (Bob Johnson)

Chapter 4:
Rooftop Garage Garden (Dean Snyder)
Rooftop Garage Garden (Dean Snyder)
Rooftop Garden (Adrián Martínez)

Chapter 5:
Balcony Garden (Dean Snyder)
Balcony Trellis (Michael Valdez)
Porch Garden (Dean Snyder)
Modular Garden (Dean Snyder)
Modular Containers (Dean Snyder)

Chapter 6:
Skylight Garden (Adrián Martínez)
Loft Garden (Michael Valdez)
Atrium Garden with Lights (Adrián Martínez)*
Corner Garden with Lights (Adrián Martínez)*

Chapter 7:
Greenhouses (Dean Snyder)
Patio Garden (Michael Valdez)

All Scratchboard Drawings by Michael Valdez

*Reprinted from *Plants Under Lights* (Simon & Schuster, 1975).

Contents

Introduction:
Grow What You Will

When we think of gardens we immediately think of large pieces of ground with elaborate greenery and flowers. Perhaps this was once an accurate picture, but not now. Today's gardens are more and more becoming gardens to accommodate *our* needs, not land's needs. Modern methods and materials enable us to garden even without much land. Now you can grow vegetables, fruit trees, annuals and perennials, house plants—all plants. It is a matter of knowing (1) where to grow plants, (2) how to grow plants, and (3) what to grow plants in. If you want a garden (even if you live in an apartment), you can have one, indoors or out. How? First scout the indoor area to see what space is available for your greenery. If your apartment or home is large, consider a skylight garden (atrium) within a room. Or do you have some loft space? Gardens in loft area above living or dining rooms can almost become indoor greenhouses. If a garden within a room is out of the question and indoor space is limited (and many times it is), how about window greenhouses and window gardens? These areas are becoming more than plant-on-the-sill setups.

If there is absolutely no space within your home, look outdoors, to the rooftops, that is, any flat surface on a roof—a garage, a shed, the house itself—any area which can carry the weight. A roof area can be very small but still suitable for a vegetable garden or a few fruit trees. Think vertically and you can create a garden in the air that will offer much pleasure.

If your outdoor area is confined to a narrow passageway (say, 8 or 10 feet clearance) and you want a garden, consider a small lean-to greenhouse. These structures require very little space and can accommodate many plants. They are really no-land gardens, and if your outdoor area is a solid block of concrete (usually called a patio by imaginative contractors), you still can have a place for plants. Patios properly enclosed (or partially enclosed) make handsome greeneries.

All kinds of gardens are possible today, with little or no land, and you can do it by using planters, packaged soil, common sense, and whatever space is available.

You need not be a carpenter or landscape architect nor a city planner—all you need is a hammer, lumber, nails, and this book in hand to build your own garden.

J.K.

Beyond the House Plant

1. Where Does Your Garden Grow?

Gardening is no longer only for people with property or backyards. Today there are many ways to have interior gardens, even within the space limitations of a small apartment. Window gardens, shelf gardens, window greenhouses, and loft and skylight gardens are all possible. If outdoor space is minimal, consider a rooftop or garage-top garden. How about that porch or balcony as a place for plants? Or perhaps a small greenhouse or enclosed patio? Let us take an overall look at the various kinds of gardens and how to get them started.

Window Space

No matter what kind of windows there are in your home—double-hung, casement, or floor-to-ceiling—you can create a setup that will accommodate plants. Exposure is unimportant because there are plants for all situations; you can even grow orchids at a north window. More important than the exposure and the plants is the *type* of window garden you design. Do not just settle for shelves at windows; there is more to a window garden than this. Extend the window into the home and create a shadowbox frame. This gives you more room for more plants and also provides places for hanging plants (from the top and at the sides). Or try a greenhouse in a window. If you have a floor-to-ceiling window wall, enclose it with glass panels parallel to the window to create an elegant gallery garden brimming with all kinds of plants. Also consider a casement window with side trellises for a unique garden where luxuriant vines clothe the walls and provide a lush greenery.

All these window treatments can be built inexpensively in a weekend; the accompanying drawings will get you started. The window garden need not be the stereotyped garden of yesterday; it can be a contemporary greenery that will beautify the home. By using specially made or do-it-yourself planter boxes as containers, you can very successfully grow plants in any of these window arrangements and without any land at all. (See Chapter 3 for a full discussion of window gardens and window greenhouses.)

Floor-to-ceiling windows offer a fine place for a no-land garden because there is ample light for plants. Standard clay pots, plastic ones, and hanging baskets are used to create the garden; the trellis screen creates the private garden look. All kinds of plants grow here: ivy geranium, begonia, orchids, philodendron, and a large dizygotheca. Additional light is furnished by skylight at left. (Photo by Gamma Photo.)

Window Gardens   The window garden relies on average home temperatures, which are fine for most plants; 72 to 78° F by day and 63 to 68° F at night. Humidity in the average home is 20 to 30 percent, a safe figure for many plants. The exposure of the window—north, south, east, west—also has some bearing; a south or east window is preferable to a north or west exposure. However, in most exposures all of the following plants will grow:

Begonias
Bromeliads
Cacti and succulents
Gesneriads
Orchids

This attractive window garden required no special equipment or carpentry. Plants in pots are on stands. Here very large plants such as the dieffenbachia at right and fern at left provide a frame for the smaller plants on stands. (Photo by Gamma Photo.)

An L-shaped window setup becomes a veritable greenery with all kinds of foliage plants: cissus, ferns, begonias, ficus. The plants are set on gravel in a metal trough, and the result is really quite attractive. (Photo by Molly Adams.)

Window Greenhouses   This situation—an enclosed unit—offers a big choice of plants and is governed only by the size of the window. Temperature, humidity, and ventilation can be controlled by opening or closing doors or panels of the greenhouse, so conditions are almost ideal for growing plants within this type of garden setup. In addition to the plants mentioned for the window garden, you can also grow:

> Midget vegetables
> Herbs
> Bulbs

House Plants   House plants are the backbone of a window or greenhouse window garden. Today there are so many good and bad indoor plants that you should know something about them before you try to grow plants at windows. For example, ferns just will not thrive at windows because they like moist and shady places. Thus you want the right plants in the right places so they prosper and give beauty, not trouble.

Begonias, a large group of plants, are stalwart indoor performers used to the rigors of dry apartments and forgetful owners.

By taking space from the passageway a handsome garden is created. Azaleas at floor level and ferns combine to provide color and beauty. The large sliding doors help control humidity and ventilation, and the latticework ceiling affords good light for plants. A unique no-land garden. (Photo by Max Eckert; Wm. Chidester, Interior Designer.)

Bromeliads are another good group of window plants. Bromeliads are really low-care plants that offer incredibly colorful foliage and are almost impossible to kill, even if you are Mr. or Ms. Brown Thumb. Most plants in the bromeliad group have strap-shaped multicolored leaves (some with small spines at the edges). Aechmeas, billbergias, vrieseas, neoregelias, and nidulariums are only a few of the plants in this vast family.

Bromeliads are more or less vase-shaped; the vases (cups) store water for the plants. Plants grow to medium height, about 30 inches. At windows you are restricted to small or medium plants, so bromeliads fit in very well.

Gesneriads are another group of plants that do well near windows. Gesneriads, relatives of the popular African violets, include kohlerias, columneas, aeschynanthus, and gloxinias. These plants require somewhat more attention than bromeliads or begonias, but they are worth the extra effort because they bear such beautiful flowers. Gesneriads reach about 24 inches in height. An accepted house plant today is the orchid. The orchid family consists of tough but beautiful plants that were once considered unsuitable for indoor growing. Not so today. Most orchids are easily grown indoors because they have pseudobulbs, so if you forget to water plants for a few days, they will still survive. Orchids are so easy that once you start growing them, you are liable to forget about other house plants!

For window or greenhouse gardens, do not forget the vast family of cacti and succulents. There are thousands of these easy-to-grow plants, and all will make any window garden sing with color. And contrary to most authorities, cacti do bloom indoors. Even the smallest parodias or rebutias (only 2 inches across) bear mammoth 5-inch flowers.

Most gardeners ignore bulbous plants, but they grow well in a window garden and should be given consideration. Lovely plants such as vallotas, with their bright red blooms, eucomis, with plumes of green flowers, and eucharis, with dazzling white flowers, have been overlooked. Yet with bulbs all the work has been done for you by Mother Nature. The flowers are already in the bulbs, just waiting for moisture and light to bring them forth. Herbs, which have many uses, are also suitable for window greenhouses and window gardens. (See Chapter 3 for a detailed discussion of plants.)

Loft and Skylight Gardens

My last home had a loft above the living room, a sort of indoor balcony. The loft area was 8 feet wide by 20 feet long. For a while it served as a small sitting room, but with some modification the loft became an indoor greenery that always drew comments from guests. I made the transition by enclosing the front of the loft with a double pair of sliding glass doors and adding planter boxes and tubs and decorative containers. I installed track lighting to furnish light and had a verdant greenery within a year. (At one time I had over a hundred house plants in this arboreal greenery.) The total cost of construction was $400.

The loft garden, whether over the living or dining room, adds a great dimension to the home and is an attractive and unique green garden. It provides a type of greenhouse in the home in relatively little and

This distinctive skylight garden is beautifully executed. The built-in planter bin and shelf afford space for philodendrons and a fine Ficus lyrata at right. Smaller trailing plants on the shelf complement the large plants, and the skylight provides ample light for plants. (Photo by Hedrich-Blessing.)

otherwise useless space. Even lofts no wider than 5 feet can become gardens with some thoughtful planning and building.

Skylight gardens, sometimes called atriums, are interior gardens that require more time and money than the other no-land gardens we have discussed. But none are out of reach of the average homeowner. The key to success is suitable top light in the form of plastic domes or glass skylights. This involves roof construction, which can be costly but is not exorbitant.

In loft and skylight gardens, you can grow large tree-type plants; there is no restriction as to height of plants like that in window gardens. The following plants would be suitable for these gardens:

An island effect is used for this lovely atrium skylight garden where sunshine floods the plants from above. Ferns and alocasias thrive. Smaller plants are in the soil in metal troughs. A fine example of no-land gardening. (Photo by Hort-Pix.)

Dieffenbachias

Dracaenas

Ferns

Ficus

Philodendrons

Palms

Other large house plants

See Chapter 6 for a more detailed discussion of loft and skylight gardens and plants for them.

Tree-Type (Specimen) Plants
Indoor trees are very popular and used frequently in rooms for accent and decoration. These plants are the mainstay of the loft or skylight (or atrium) garden. The larger decorator plants are impressive and create beauty within any room. There are some outdoor trees (field-grown) that will adapt to indoor growing, but most specimen plants are the familiar house plants like dracaenas and dieffenbachias, grown to tree shape. You can buy these plants already shaped, or train your own through the years by trimming off bottom growth and training the plant to a specific growth pattern. Scheffleras can be trained to a lovely branching form; *Dracaena marginata* can achieve a sculpturesque appearance; and *Crassula argentea* and *Pittosporum tobira* will be bushy if trained correctly.

In any case, once established, tree-type or specimen plants require large containers and frequent feeding. The food replenishes nutrients that the plant uses. You should not repot trees very often because the shock is too great to the plant, so a sensible feeding program will ensure success with these plants. (Specimen plants are discussed in detail in Chapter 6.)

Rooftop, Balcony, and Porch Gardens
An outdoor garden can be built on the roof of a garage, house, or even a shed. As long as the structure can support the weight of plants and containers, a garden in the air need not cost a fortune. More construction is necessary for the roof garden than for a window or loft arrangement, but the rewards are far greater. Actual construction can be done a little at a time, and because no foundation is needed, you can do most of the work yourself. Planters and containers, the most vital parts of your roof garden, and suitable railings and screens will transform a useless roof into a beautiful outdoor garden at very little cost. (A very serviceable garden can be built for less than $500.)

Many new apartment buildings have balcony areas; old apartments have porches. These outdoor places should not be neglected. Arrange containers and boxes with plants to make an inexpensive balcony/porch garden. You can also add some trellis screens; grow beautiful and dramatic vines on the trellises to dress up the balcony or porch. Balconies of contemporary apartments provide an additional living/garden area that can be very handsome. Even if balconies are small or narrow (and they usually are), don't leave them bare, because they look too vacant and detract from the total apartment or living space.

Depending on size, rooftop, balcony, and porch gardens can accommodate plants like:

Annuals and perennials
Vegetables
Fruit trees
Trees and shrubs
Decorative vines

In Chapters 4 and 5 we explore the joys of these gardens in the air.

Vegetables A few vegetables—tomatoes, cucumbers—can be grown indoors, but most vegetables must be grown outside. (Most vegetables need the sun and heat that only outdoor conditions can provide, so indoor growing is really not practical.) For rooftops, balconies, and porches there is a wide variety of vegetables, from squash to lettuce and beans, that you can grow and enjoy eating.

Growing vegetables on rooftops or in other outdoor areas provides plants with almost perfect conditions: there is excellent light and good air ventilation. However, just what you grow will depend on your local climate. Vegetables are either cool-season (for example, cauliflower and brussels sprouts) or warm-season (tomatoes and eggplant). But even within these limitations there are certain varieties of vegetables that will adapt or are specially bred for certain areas; these varieties are available at nurseries.

You can grow vegetables from seed (and it is fun), but if time is of the essence, grow prestarts. Prestarts are seedlings that already have been germinated; they are sold during the proper season. Set prestarts directly into planters for continued growing outdoors.

Vines Vines—clematis, bougainvillea, and dozens of others—offer the lazy gardener an easy way to have cascading greenery in a short time. And this lush, usually dense growth can hide unsightly areas as well as furnish a great deal of foliage from two or three plants. In addition, vines also provide vertical color so necessary in most gardens. So for decorative value, function, and beauty, vines are tough to beat.

Basically, these are easy plants to grow; they require deep holes when planting them and a rich soil, and then plenty of water. Vines usually grow very quickly, so abundant moisture is necessary. You can grow them in the ground or in planter boxes and use vines where they will do the most for the garden; that is, place them strategically so they are used to the fullest. Good locations are against walls or fences or any area where a vertical accent is needed.

Generally, trellis supports are necessary for vines so they can be trained and pruned to pattern (informal or formal) and do not become a jungle of leaves.

This simple rooftop garden relies on pot plants and while it is not lush, there is still a nice green feeling about it.

Trees and Shrubs

Any rooftop garden needs a few ornamental trees and shrubs for definition and beauty. And trees and shrubs often complement larger balconies and porches. The kind of plant you decide to grow will depend on your individual climate, but there are trees and shrubs for all regions. Remember that plants available at local suppliers are generally those plants that are most adaptable to your weather. (You are not, however, restricted to these plants.)

Some of the dwarf fruit trees can be part of your garden-in-the-air, too. Nectarines and peaches, for example, and citrus of all kinds do very well in rooftop and balcony gardens. However, the most serious problem will be space: there never will be enough room to grow everything you want, so you will have to be somewhat selective.

In Chapter 4 you will find a list of trees of many kinds for roof and balcony gardening.

Annuals and Perennials

Most annuals and perennials need outdoor conditions, that is, rooftop, balcony, or porch gardens. Annuals and perennials are perfect for seasonal color and are the easiest of plants to grow: all they need are good sunlight and lots of water. Group these plants in pots to create a colorful display, an integral part of the roof garden. (There are extensive lists of annuals and perennials in Chapter 5.)

Greenhouse and Patio Gardens

Greenhouses offer a world of gardening because they give you maximum gardening in minimum space. (You need only 6 to 8 feet of space to construct a greenhouse.) The greenhouse also adds a distinctive note to your home and lets you grow many kinds of plants, from orchids to vegetables. There are so many plant possibilities for the outdoor greenhouse (what we also call a lean-to) that you may spend too many hours gardening!

Whether 4 x 6 feet or 8 x 10 feet, a greenhouse creates a green world you can enjoy 365 days a year. Under controlled conditions, you can grow

An attached greenhouse is still another way to have plants where there is little or no land. Flowering plants abound, making this a pleasant place to sit and enjoy nature. (Photo by Lorriane Burgess.)

A patio garden that brings indoors and outdoors together with ease. There is a built-in planter bed, and vines on the wall furnish the decorative accent to make this patio a really beautiful area. (Photo by Ken Molino.)

many many plants, or simply use the greenhouse as a special place for house plants. The greenhouse can be filled with orchids or begonias or be a starting place for annuals and perennials. In fact, you can grow so many different plants that your selection is unlimited; this is why no list is included here.

Patios are almost always small, about 8 x 8 feet, and consist when first built of just a cement slab adjacent to the rear of your house. But you can turn these areas into delightful greeneries by the use of trellises or fences. You can hang plants, stack plants, and so on, in the patio. You will not be able to have a jungle because your overall area will remain small, but you can grow a garden of colorful beauty.

Patio areas can be beautiful with suitable plants and again the problem is which plants to grow. You will have to pick and choose because you cannot grow everything in a confined area. If you want cut flowers, use annuals and perennials, but if you favor flavor you might want to grow some of your own vegetables. You can also make your patio a place for tropical plants with gaudy flowers if that is your preference. No matter what kind of patio garden you decide on, always include a few tubbed trees and shrubs to provide balance and scale to the area. (Greenhouse and patio gardens are discussed fully in Chapter 7.)

2. What Does Your Garden Grow In?

In Chapter 1 we discussed the various types of no-land gardens. Now we will consider what your plants will grow in. Because containers are so important in no-land gardening, we will cover both those containers you buy and those you make.

Soil, taken for granted in outdoor gardening, deserves special mention because plants need soil to grow in. And because plants in containers are confined to housings, they use up the soil's nutrients. These nutrients must be replaced after a time with additional food (plant fertilizers).

Containers

New materials and methods of manufacturing have made containers much more exciting than they used to be. Besides redwood, there are now attractive clay, metal, or concrete containers in a range of sizes and shapes: round, square, rectangular, contoured, and tapered. Bronze-gilt pots, elegant rattan planters, wrought iron pedestals are all part of today's parade of containers. Plastic tubs and tempered-glass containers are also available. There is virtually no end to the kind of pot, tub, or box you can buy or make.

Terra-Cotta Containers

The standard terra-cotta pot (an excellent container), is now available in many sizes and shapes. Today, these pots come in these designs:

Italian pots: The border is modified to a tight lip. Some pots have round edges, others are beveled, and some are rimless.

Venetian pots: Barrel-shaped containers with concentric bands pressed into the sides.

Spanish pots: These have outwardly flared sides and flared lips and heavier walls than conventional pots.

Bulb pans: Bowls, generally less than half as high as wide. They look like deep saucers.

Azalea or fern pots: Squat, and low containers.

Cylindrical pots: Handsome, straight-sided, and rimless cylinders.

Miscellaneous: Strawberry jars, miniature donkeys, chickens.

Rectangular pots: Very handsome. Generally have outside designs.

Square pots: Good-looking but heavy.

Glazed, Plastic, and Cachepot Containers

With glazed containers you have the advantage of selecting a specific color rather than being restricted to the terra-cotta color. The glazed pots also have a shiny finish that imparts elegance, and today these pots often come with drainage holes (years ago they did not).

Plastic pots also come in many sizes and colors. Do avoid the light-weight—or flexible—pots because if you put large plants in them, the pots will tip over. However, rigid plastic pots, with heavy walls, are satisfactory, and the clear acrylic pots are most handsome at windows. Remember that plastic, fiberglass, or acrylic containers will hold water longer than clay pots.

Very attractive containers that look good in a window garden are cachepots. Cachepots were originally designed as colorful coverups for flowerpots, but plants can be put directly into them. These decorative containers come in many sizes, shapes, and materials. The porcelain cachepots, generally splashed with fruit or flower designs, and the hexagonal pots are expecially pleasing.

Saucers

Now most containers come with suitable saucers to catch excess water. If a pot does not have a matching saucer, buy any saucer, because water stains on windowsills and glass surfaces are awful looking. Saucers come in terra cotta, plastic, or acrylic. Choose the ones most appropriate for the pots you are using.

Wood Containers

Commercially made containers are fine for plants, but it is more prudent to make your own planting tubs and boxes. The attractive no-land garden depends on custom-made planters that fit specific areas, so you will have to take hammer and nails in hand. But do not panic; the planters are not hard to make, and you will be saving money. (Explicit construction data are discussed in Chapter 9.)

For a 12-inch box, 1 x 12-inch redwood stock is best. To give the box a finished appearance, stain it a dark color and then nail 1 x 1-inch strips spaced ½ inch apart around it. For variation, cap the box with a 2-inch molding on the top and at corner seams. Larger boxes can be made from 2-inch redwood stock. Be sure to drill drainage holes (½ inch in diameter) in the bottoms of boxes.

CLAY POTS

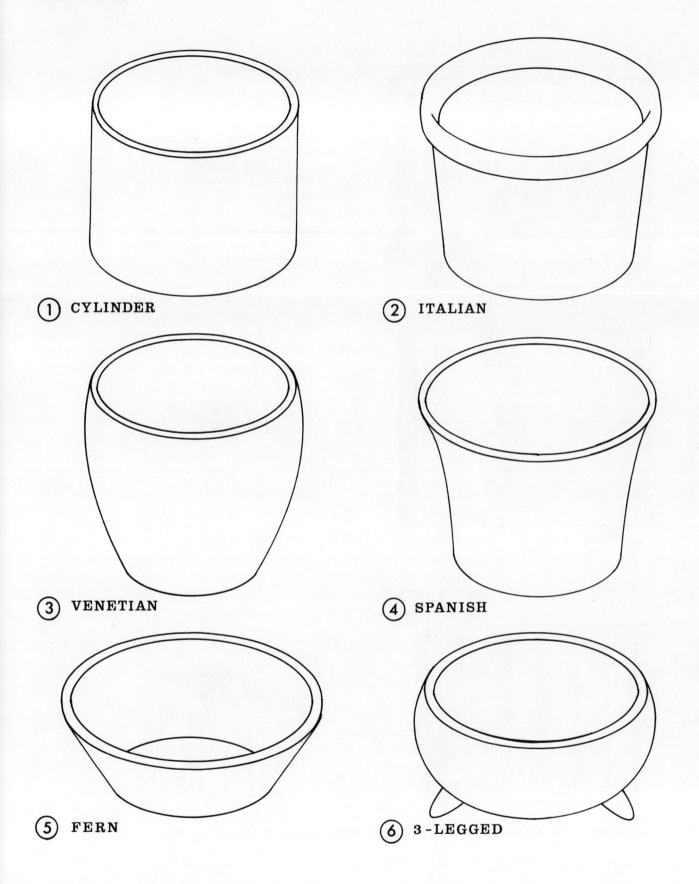

① CYLINDER

② ITALIAN

③ VENETIAN

④ SPANISH

⑤ FERN

⑥ 3-LEGGED

PLANTER BOXES

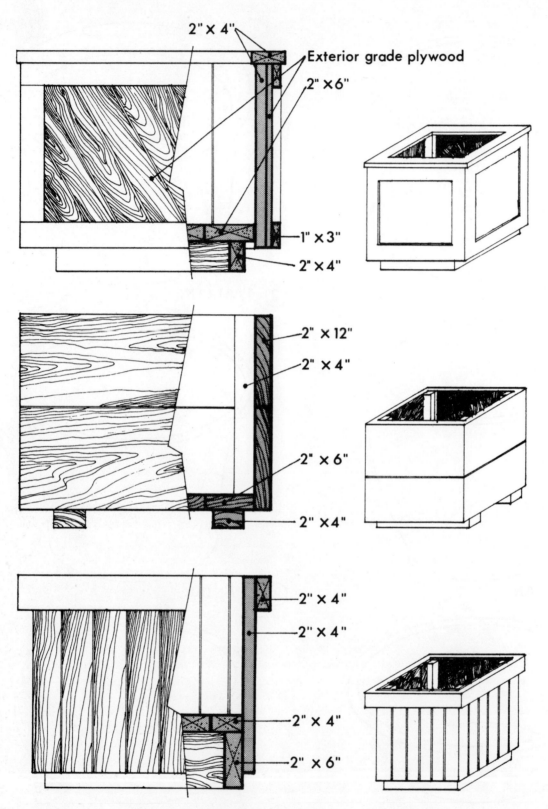

2" × 4"

Exterior grade plywood

2" ×6"

1" × 3"

2" × 4"

2" × 12"

2" × 4"

2" × 6"

2" × 4"

2" × 4"

2" × 4"

2" × 4"

2" × 6"

Lumber: pine, redwood, cedar; box dimensions: personal specs.

You can make your own garden by using 2 x 12 redwood and stacking boxes to save space. This 4 x 8 foot growing area will accommodate many kinds of plants. (Photo by author.)

In this photo, plants have started growing to provide a lovely small garden in a confined area. (Photo by author.)

Redwood is the basic wood for planters and tubs because it resists decay, lasts for years, is easy to work with, weathers beautifully if unpainted, or can be painted. Use construction grade redwood, or, if a really elegant touch is necessary, kiln-dried heart construction redwood (this is more expensive). Standard planter boxes are simply four sides and a bottom. They are long and low, rectangularly shaped. You can make narrow boxes, say 6 inches wide, or larger boxes, 24 inches wide. With smaller boxes, a depth of 6 to 8 inches is best; larger ones can be up to 24 inches deep. Use these planters along walls, stacked, or in various other arrangements to create a mass effect of plants.

Square redwood boxes are popular because, like modular furniture, they can be used in an array of designs. You can stack them, butt them together, or whatever, to create lush displays of greenery while adding much attractiveness to an area. These modular boxes should correlate with the space; there should be balance and symmetry, to create a total picture in the garden. For a 12-inch cube, use 1 x 12-inch redwood. (See the end of Chapter 5 for more about modular gardening.)

Soil   Soil is important to all plants—indoors and outdoors—but it is especially vital in no-land gardening, where most plants are confined to containers. Without a soil that has adequate nutrients, plants simply cannot grow. And without a soil that has enough porosity for air to circulate through the soil, plants will not readily grow either. Such soil becomes compacted and caked and is virtually useless to plants.

What is a good soil? It is one that is mealy and porous, never too sandy or too clayey. Soil must have air spaces so water and air can pass through it. Often good soils smell good; they have a pleasant humusy odor.

Standard clay pots make fine containers for plants; pots come in many sizes and designs now.

Handsome terra-cotta decorative planters and pots are also available and work well for no-land gardens. Because there are so many containers available today, pick and choose carefully.

Bulk soil is not always available, but if you can find it, use it. Bulk soil is usually your best buy; this is the soil that florists or nurseries use for planting because it contains all necessary ingredients. However, today most soils are sold in either small packages or large 50-pound bags. Forget the small hobby sacks because there is only enough soil in them for three or four plants.

It is difficult to determine what is in the soil you buy in 50-pound bags because contents are not marked on the bags. It is a question of hit-or-miss or taking your nurseryman's suggestion. To play it safe, add some humus or compost (sold in small packages) to be sure the soil has good tilth (porosity) and nutrients.

The ultimate best buy in soil for quality and quantity is bulk soil delivered by the truckload usually 5 cubic yards. This soil is purchased from large nurseries and is screened and specially prepared. I use it for my gardens whenever I can get it (it *is* hard to get).

Wooden planters such as this may not be very decorative but they do accommodate many plants and work well for small gardens; they define the perimeter of the garden area and create balance. (Photo by Matthew Barr.)

Manures and Composts

Manures are a great source of nitrogen, which is essential to plant health. Compost or humus (also called leaf mold) is what makes soil good soil. It is decayed vegetable matter that builds up on forest floors; it is the combined product of many natural materials—leaves, limbs, twigs—that have rotted. (Humus also contains the dung of large and small animals.) Plants constantly use up humus, even if the original packaged soil had it at the start, so eventually you have to add humus to your soil. You can buy humus or make your own by having a compost heap. However, most people with no-land gardens do not have the space necessary for a compost heap, so the best bet is to buy the packaged humus and add it to the soil.

How much humus and how much compost should you add to soil? The amounts depend on the size of the container, so all I can suggest is that you add a little at a time. Run your hands through the soil; when it has good porosity and feels mealy like a well-done baked potato, you have added sufficient quantities of both ingredients.

There are also soilless mixes that contain a conglomerate of ingredients. Soilless mixes are becoming popular for container plants, but it is a chore to care for plants in these mixes because you must constantly feed plants, which is expensive and time-consuming. Growers use the soilless mixes because they are lightweight, but for the average no-land gardener they are more a curse than a blessing.

Feeding

Plants confined to containers, as they are in no-land gardening, will need feeding after a few months because most nutrients in the soil will have been depleted. There are dozens of different plant foods (fertilizers) sold, so it is wise to know just what plant foods are all about.

Fertilizers contain nitrogen, to encourage foliage growth; phosphorous, to stimulate good stem growth; and potassium, to help make the plant strong. These elements are marked on the bottle or package in that order, in percentages. For example, a plant food marked 10-10-5 means that it contains 10 percent nitrogen, 10 percent phosphorous, and 5 percent potassium. (The remainder is filler.) For all practical purposes, 10-10-5 is an excellent all-around plant food because it is neither so strong as to cause leaf burn nor so weak as to be ineffective.

Fertilizers also vary in form. The most practical to use is the granular type, which you just scatter on the soil and then apply water to. Soluble and foliar plant foods have to be mixed with water. There is also a systemic feeding/insecticide food; this product does two things at once: it keeps away insects and feeds plants.

Plant foods are necessary, so know the rules about when and how to apply them to best help your plants:

1. *Do not feed an ailing plant; it cannot absorb food.*
2. *Do not feed plants when they are resting (usually in winter).*
3. *Do not try to force a plant into growth with excessive feeding.*
4. *Be sure soil is moist before adding plant food.*
5. *Feed plants during active growth, usually in spring and summer.*

3. Window Gardens

The best light for plants in the apartment or home is at a window, which is why so many gardeners use window areas for their plants. But there is another factor involved: plants at windows look good and add colorful beauty to a room. For a long time most people just placed a few pot plants at windows and that was it, but today you can create all kinds of handsome arrangements and beauty with merely a little thought and planning.

The window garden may be simply a row of potted plants on shelves and windowsills or a more elaborate garden with hanging plants, plants in brackets, plants on stands, and so on. The idea is to first formulate some sort of balanced setup. For example, if you want a simple window garden, use the same type of pots in the same size or similar pots of various sizes. Either way you will create a totally balanced, pleasing picture. If you want a shelf garden, be sure shelves are wide enough to accommodate pots. For a hanging window garden, use sturdy ceiling hangers and decorative baskets or pots. In other words, plan ahead for your delightful window garden.

Plan and Design

Do not just set a few potted plants on window shelves and expect a total garden; it does *not* work. First appraise the window as to size, height, and width. Forget shelves for a moment and visualize a complete scene, like a picture you might paint. What goes where? What size plants? What kind of pots? Do you need height with tall plants or a bushy effect with low growers? Consider vines and trailers.

Now draw a rough sketch of the area and jot in forms and masses. You need not be an artist to do this. Even the roughest of sketches will, when it is finished, have some meaning with the forms and figures. For example, use a light gray for small plants, dark gray for medium growers, and black for tall plants. The values of the markings will indicate if the window is balanced and if it will look good once installed.

If the window is very small, say a standard 24 x 30 inches, do not try to

PLANTER BOX GARDEN

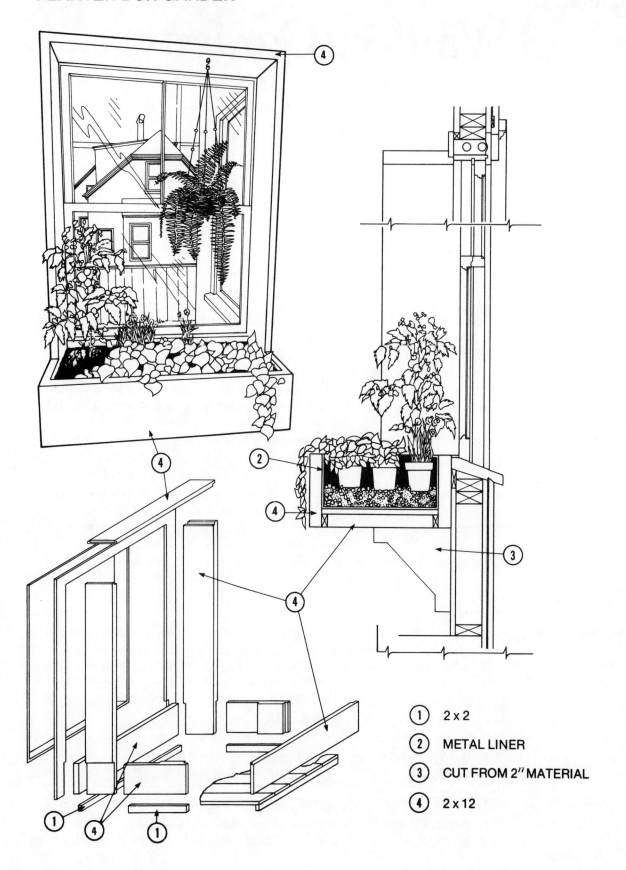

① 2 x 2

② METAL LINER

③ CUT FROM 2″ MATERIAL

④ 2 x 12

SHELF GARDEN

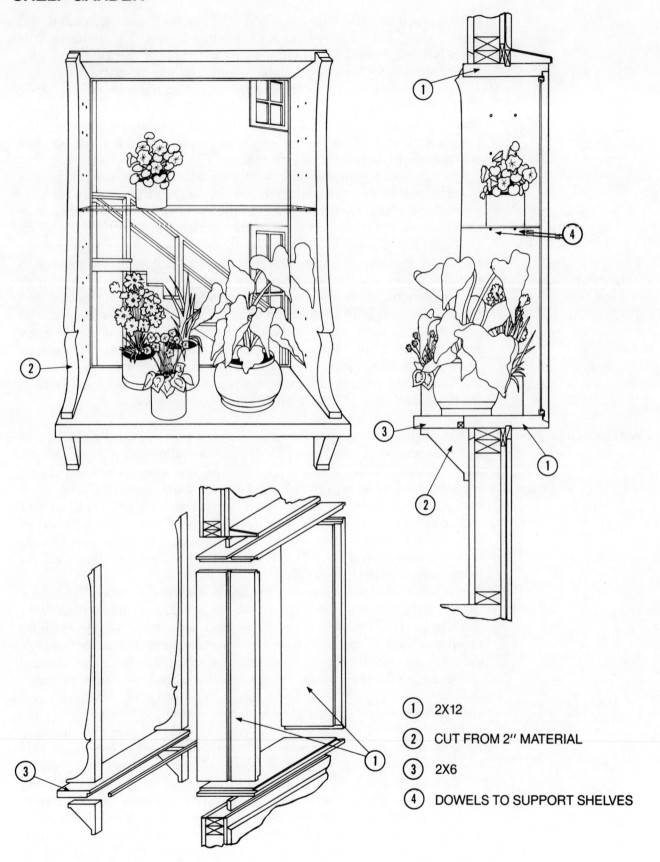

1 2X12

2 CUT FROM 2" MATERIAL

3 2X6

4 DOWELS TO SUPPORT SHELVES

do too much to it. The best solution is to extend the sides, bottom, and top by using 2 x 12 boards in a shadowbox design. This requires little space but will "open" the window, giving you space at the top for hanging plants, at the sides for pots in brackets, and a sill to hold pots.

An old-fashioned double-hung window has ample side and top space for the hanging of plants. Place simple glass shelves across the window, bracing each end of the shelf with wooden blocks. For an added decoration, install some trellis on the wall at each side to broaden the window and provide space for climbing plants.

Floor-to-ceiling windows are another challenge. You can merely set potted plants at the base of the window, but it might pay you to consider extending the area to include some of the room space and installing glass panels in wooden frames parallel to the windows to provide more space. If you do use glass panels, protect the floor from water stain (unless it is a tile floor) by using custom-made metal pans. Either fill the pans with gravel as a base for the pots or plant directly in them. Again, as with all garden designs, draw a sketch and consider both the horizontal and vertical elements of the design and what kind of plants you will need.

Bay windows offer the best area for a garden because you can do many things to create the welcome verdant feeling. Use a few suspension-type plant poles within the bay area to provide more space for plants.

Do not forget that suitable containers and floor housings must be used for plants and water. These items will be discussed later.

Window Greenhouses

Although the window is the most accepted place for indoor plants, it is also the most overlooked area as a place for a real greenery: a greenhouse. (Note: do not confuse window greenhouses, which are indoor structures, with the outdoor lean-to greenhouses discussed in Chapter 7.) With some minor modifications the window can become an excellent enclosed area with controlled conditions where many kinds of plants can flourish. In the enclosed area it is easy to regulate temperature and humidity; conditions are almost ideal for all kinds of plants. Also, because plants will be in one area, watering will be easy.

Just what kind of window greenhouse you make depends on four factors: (1) whether you own your own home, (2) how many plants you want to grow, (3) what kind of plants you want to grow, and (4) how much you want to spend. The window greenhouse can be made inside of existing windows. But for more elaborate structures, remove the window and frame so the greenhouse extends outside as well as inside. In either case, the face of the greenhouse is angled and made of glass in frames, with opening and closing facilities for air circulation.

To make a window greenhouse from an existing window (an easy project), the main construction involves frames for glass and glazing. (If you would rather not tackle this yourself, buy commercially preglazed windows at building supply houses.) To allow air to enter the growing area, merely hinge the frames; it is then easy to open and close the frames. Our drawing shows a basic window greenhouse. The greenhouse can be fitted to an existing window; or the greenhouse can extend outside, which

PYRAMID WINDOW GREENHOUSE

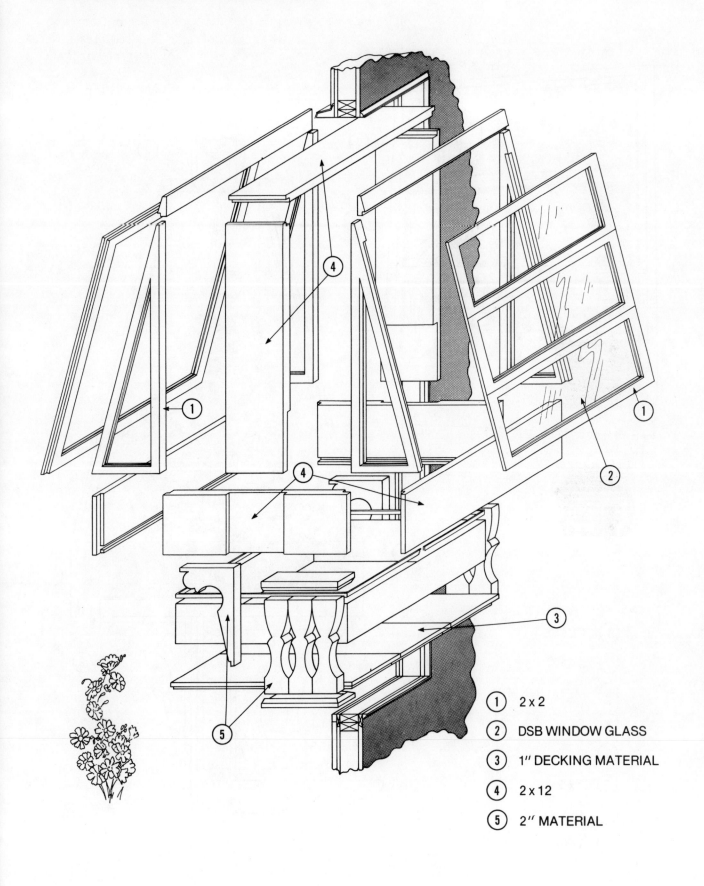

(1) 2 x 2

(2) DSB WINDOW GLASS

(3) 1" DECKING MATERIAL

(4) 2 x 12

(5) 2" MATERIAL

PYRAMID WINDOW GREENHOUSE

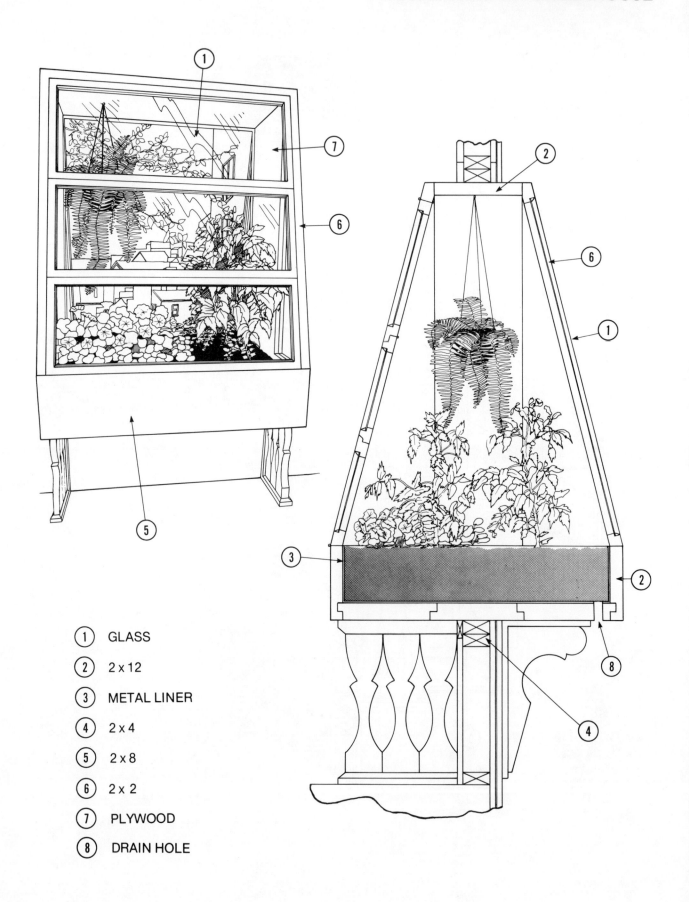

1. GLASS
2. 2 x 12
3. METAL LINER
4. 2 x 4
5. 2 x 8
6. 2 x 2
7. PLYWOOD
8. DRAIN HOLE

REMOVING A WINDOW

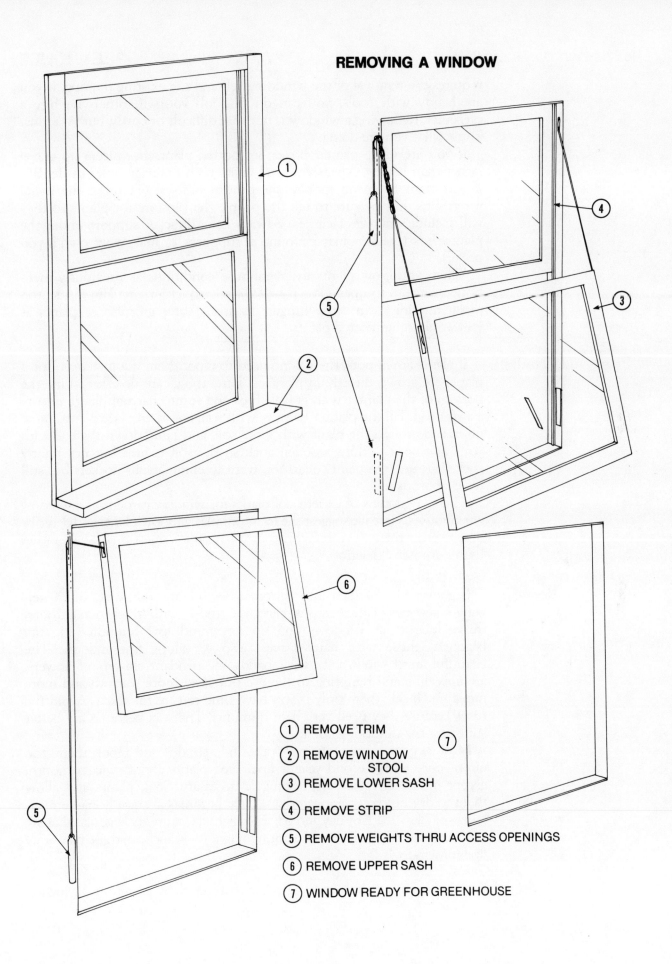

1. REMOVE TRIM
2. REMOVE WINDOW STOOL
3. REMOVE LOWER SASH
4. REMOVE STRIP
5. REMOVE WEIGHTS THRU ACCESS OPENINGS
6. REMOVE UPPER SASH
7. WINDOW READY FOR GREENHOUSE

requires the removal of the window itself and the existing framing. If you are handy with tools, you can do this job yourself; otherwise hire a carpenter. Removing a window is not that difficult or costly, but you must know what you are doing.

If you are using planter boxes, set potted plants in saucers on gravel rather than having expensive metal liners with drainage holes made. But if you want to spend money, sheet-metal houses will make the metal insert bins. Just be sure to tell the people the bins are for plants so they will include drainage facilities. Always use a bracket support under the planter box (brackets may be found at suppliers, or make your own if you prefer).

When you grow plants in greenhouse conditions as previously mentioned, be sure to open glass panels slightly to let air circulate inside; too much humidity can cause fungus diseases. Water greenhouse plants as you would other potted plants.

Plants and Planting

If plants are in pots, there is no need to repot them the first year. But if plants are grown directly in planters, some things are necessary. Line the bottom of the planter with gravel chips and some charcoal bits to ensure a sweet soil. Fill the planter halfway with soil, and then place plants. Now fill in and around the plant with more soil, and tamp down the soil with your fingers or a blunt wooden stick so the soil is firm but not tightly packed around the plant collar. You want to eliminate air pockets but still have a porous soil.

There are dozens of varieties of plants for window gardens and window greenhouses. Here we suggest the most popular window plants and describe how to grow them. If your favorite is missing, it is a question of space rather than purposeful deletion.

Begonias

Begonias are classified into rhizomatous, hirsute, rex, wax, and angel-wing categories. Rhizomatous begonias (those with thick aerial roots) thrive indoors at windows and do not mind low humidity. Hirsute begonias (those with hairy leaves) also get along fine indoors. The beautiful angel wings, with their handsome pendant clusters of flowers, are appealing and tempting to the eye but need more warmth and more moisture. Tackle them only if you have time to care for them. Avoid the rexes because they need very high humidity. The wax begonias are better suited for the outdoor garden.

Most begonias enjoy being potbound, so do not repot them too often—once every second year is fine. Feed plants about twice a month, except in winter, when no feeding is necessary. Soak plants and allow them to dry out between waterings. Give begonias average home temperatures of 72 to 78° F by day and 68° F at night. Here are six begonias that are not very large (they reach a maximum height of 36 inches); these plants are fine for windows.

Begonia boweri (eye-lash begonia). A charming plant, to about 30 inches, with delicate green leaves stitched with black. Very decorative and worthy of a place in any window.

B. 'Alleryi.' Frosted green leaves accented with purple; pale pink flowers.

B. 'Cleopatra.' Exquisite foliage plant; leaves splashed with gold, brown, and chartreuse. Good window plant.

B. 'Crestabruchi.' A magnificent plant with yellow-green ruffled leaves.

B. *erythrophylla* (beefsteak begonia). Lovely light green round leaves. Robust.

B. *luxurians.* Erect stems carry compounds of large leaves; treelike growth. Nice accent.

A handsome array of plants is arranged in a floor-to-ceiling window area. A large poinsettia is at the left, a palm on the right, and hanging baskets of tradescantia complete the window (or alcove) garden. (Photo by Matthew Barr.)

With little actual construction this window space was tailor-made for plants. A tile built-in bin was used on the floor to hold plants, and hanging baskets of plants complete the handsome apartment window greenery. (Photo by Gamma Photo.)

Bromeliads   Bromeliads are superior window-garden plants with multicolored leaves and brightly colored flower bracts. There are small, medium, and large plants, so the choice is vast for window growing. Most bromeliads are vase-shaped and thus hold water in reserve in case you forget to water them.

Plants are best grown in equal parts of soil and crushed fir bark (at suppliers) and require a somewhat dry soil; the main thing is to keep the cup filled with water. In direct sun the plants will have vividly colored foliage, but they will also succeed in bright indirect light, although coloring will not be as vivid. Bromeliads adapt well to average home conditions and really require little care.

This is a vast group of plants, so I can only touch on some of them.

Aechmea fasciata. A vase-shaped plant with green leaves with transverse white bands. Handsome.

Billbergia. Many species in this genus. Most are tubular-shaped and have vividly colored foliage.

Neoregelia tricolor. A handsome rosette-shaped plant with multicolored leaves.

Nidularium. Many species in this group. Most have a rosette shape and handsome colored leaves.

Vriesea splendens. Small plant, to 24 inches, with apple-green leaves.

Guzmania lingulata. Vase-shaped plant with green leaves and handsome orange flower bracts.

Even simple shelves can make a window garden with one accent trailing plant of coleus. Nothing elaborate here but still a charming look. (Photo by Gamma Photo.)

All kinds of plants grow in a bay window; the plant stand is the central accent with other plants nicely arranged around it. Plants include Dracaena marginata at left, a ficus at floor level, cactus and a small palm at right. The hanging plant is chlorophytum. (Photo by Gamma Photo.)

Gesneriads   *Kohleria amabilis* is a flowering gesneriad that will brighten your dullest days. It is a regal plant, with upright growth and large and velvety dark green leaves. Occasionally, but not often, this plant will surprise you with some funnel-shaped pink flowers. Keep the plant reasonably moist and in good light.

Another gesneriad worthy of mention is *Columnea arguta,* a low, light, level plant that has trailing and small dark green leaves. Huge salmon-red flowers dot the plant in warm weather. Keep the plant evenly moist. Do select this trailer rather than aeschynanthus (the lipstick vine), which most dealers will try to sell you in its place.

If you have the time and patience and are fond of brightly colored foliage and beautiful flowers, try the more temperamental episcias. These lovely plants are not easy to grow because they like warmth (78° F) and humidity of 60 to 70 percent. But because they are so handsome, they are worth a try.

Gloxinias, those fabulous large flowering bulbs you see at florists', can also be grown at your window garden. Start gloxinias slowly into growth with moderate waterings, increasing moisture as plants get larger. Once leaves are full-grown, keep the soil evenly moist at all times, and put gloxinias in a bright (but not sunny) cool place (55° F). Gloxinias will not succeed in excessive heat. When flowers fade, let foliage die off and then store the bulbs in their pots in a paper sack in a cool, dry place. Start the bulbs again in about three months, repotting them in fresh soil and a fresh pot.

The most popular gesneriads are African violets. I do not mean to give them short notice here, but because there are so many books on the subject, just let me say that these shady beauties need only an evenly moist soil and rather moderate temperatures to succeed indoors. Avoid getting leaves wet or soil too damp. There are hundreds of African violet varieties, including some fine miniature types.

Here are some of the gesneriads you might want to grow:

Achimenes. These gesneriads grow from corms. Achimenes have dark green leaves and bright and flat-faced lavender, red, or yellow flowers.

Aeschynanthus lobbianus (lipstick vine). Shiny dark green leaves and brown flowers.

A. speciosus. Green leaves and trailing red flowers.

Columnea arguta. Trailing vine with pointed leaves and red-orange flowers.

C. microphylla. Trailing plant with tiny dark green leaves and vivid red flowers.

Episcia acajou. Silvery foliage and red flowers. Pendant habit.

E. lilacina. Bronze leaves and blue flowers.

Kohleria amabilis. Velvety green leaves and pink flowers with purple dots.

K. bogotensis. Speckled leaves and red and yellow blooms.

Rechsteineria cardinalis. Small plant with large velvety green leaves and scarlet tubular flowers.

Saintpaulia (African violets). Hundreds of varieties; mostly small plants with flat-faced flowers; many colors.

Smithiantha multiflora. Soft hairy leaves with red blooms.

Orchids   Orchids do grow and bloom indoors, with no more care—perhaps less—than most house plants. Most orchids have pseudobulbs, so if you forget to water them a few days they still survive. Generally, orchids are either terrestrial (earth growing) or epiphytic (airborne). The terrestrials grow in soil like most other plants. The epiphytes cling to tree branches; however, they are not parasites and do not harm their hosts.

It is best to use a special flowerpot with slots for most orchids; the openings permit air circulation around the roots. (These pots are sold at orchid nurseries.) You will also need osmunda fiber, a material derived from the root system of various ferns, or a supply of fir bark (chopped bark). Use either material by itself for the epiphytes. For the terrestrials, combine part humus, part leaf mold, and part chopped osmunda.

Pot orchids as you would any other house plant. Provide adequate drainage material, leave space on top of the soil for watering, and be sure the size of the plant is in keeping with the size of the pot. Use tepid (60 to 70° F) water. When winter heat fluctuates, so must your watering schedule. The artificial heat dries out the air, so the plants need more water. The size of the pot also affects the amount: small pots dry out quickly, large pots slowly. I cannot give more specific watering rules because each orchid must be treated individually.

Average room temperatures, 65 to 75° F, nicely accommodate most orchids. At night set the thermostat lower, to 50 to 60° F; plants at your windows, like those in nature, benefit from a 10-, to 15-degree drop in temperature. Most orchids do not need high humidity; 30 to 40 percent is fine. At night, along with lower temperatures, provide lower humidity. Orchids need some light, but most do not want scorching sun. The easy-to-grow kinds we will discuss will do fine at a west, east, or even a north window. Plants must have bottom ventilation, so set containers on strips of wood placed over clay saucers. Remember that orchids are basically air plants.

The cost of orchids ranges from $5 to $15 for mature specimens. There are dozens of suppliers throughout the country. Here are some of the best orchids for your window garden:

Aerides odoratum. Fragrant straplike leaves; pendant scapes of white-and-

A window garden is always lovely. Here is one with tiny-leaved bamboo in the corner, fern below, and a row of colorful seasonal plants at base of window. (Photo by Clark Photo/Graphic.)

pink flowers. Grows to 20 inches. Usually spring-flowering. Grow in fir bark.

Brassavola nodosa. Five-inch succulent green leaves; large and fragrant white blooms.

Cattleya skinneri. Light green leathery foliage; large lavender flowers. Summer-blooming.

Cycnoches chlorochilon. Large plant, with 7-inch chartreuse flowers shaped like a swan's neck.

Cypripedium insigne. Erect stalks of greenish blooms; typical lady-slipper type. Winter flowering.

Dendrobium nobile hybrids. Cane-type growth, many varieties; flowers are usually white, pink, and purple. Winter to spring bloom.

Epidendrum atropurpureum. Large plant, with single leathery leaves and wands of purple and pink blooms. Spring-blooming.

Lycaste aromatica. Medium-sized plant, with grasslike leaves and golden yellow fragrant flowers. October/November bloom.

Miltonia spectabilis. Large rose-colored flowers with purple lips in summer.

Oncidium ampliatum. Spring-flowering, with hundreds of small yellow and brown flowers.

Phalaenopsis amabilis. Large plant, with broad spatula-shaped leaves and long stems of open-faced white flowers.

Stanhopea oculata. Broad dark green leaves; pendant scapes of lemon yellow flowers in late summer. Grow in a basket.

Trichopilia tortilis. Unusual whitish pink, corkscrew-shaped flower. Spring and summer flowering.

Vanda caerulea. Medium-sized plant. Pale blue blooms in autumn or winter.

The window area of this kitchen was screened off from the rest of the room and a metal trough inserted, covered with white gravel. The plants are ficus species. This type of gallery or passageway garden only requires a 4-foot-wide area. (Photo courtesy Kentile Corp.)

Cacti   Most people think cacti grow in pure sand, but actually they need a good soil mix with the right nutrients, just like other plants. Which soil mixture you choose among the many available depends upon the size and type of plant you are growing. Most cacti are desert dwellers, but some, like the Christmas cactus, are native to the rain forests and thus need a different type of soil.

Use a mix of equal parts of garden loam and small pebbles for most cacti. For jungle cacti—for example, rhipsalis, schlumbergera, and zygocactus—use a mixture of one part shredded tree bark or osmunda (sold at nurseries) and one part garden loam. Mix the ingredients *thoroughly*, making sure the soil has a friable texture so it drains excess water yet retains moisture for plant roots.

Cacti generally need good light, some sun a few hours a day, to really thrive. However, even in less ideal situations they will still survive, although they will not grow as rapidly. Do not expect all your cacti to bloom unless they are in a very sunny location. Use zygocactus, rhipsalis, lobivias, parodias, and rebutias because they not only produce flowers but can, if they have to, bloom in lower light levels. Turn plants occasionally (unless they are in bud) so light evenly reaches all parts of the plant; otherwise plants will lean toward the light.

Most cacti are flexible as to temperatures, tolerating from 55 to 90° F without harm, although 75° F by day and 65° F by night is ideal. Cacti rest in winter and thus need less warmth then, so lower temperatures of 65° F by day and 55° F by night are very beneficial.

Try the following cacti in your window greenhouse:

Cephalocereus palmeri (wooly torch). This is a column-shaped plant, with short blue-green spines and tufts of white wooly hairs completely covering it. More of an oddity than a beauty.

Chamaecereus silvestri (peanut cactus). A fine branching cactus, with clusters of short, spiny green branches.

Echinocactus grusonii (golden barrel). A truly beautiful plant, the golden barrel is a symmetrical globe covered with sharp golden yellow spines; large plants (about 8 inches in diameter) are delightful decorative accents.

E. baileyi. Another good echinocactus, as easy to grow as the golden barrel, this column-shaped cactus has white spines that add a cheerful note indoors. The large flowers are bright yellow. It needs somewhat more light than most cacti.

Mammillaria bocasana (powder-puff cactus). This one has clustering growth, hooked central spines covered with thin hair, and occasionally, small and pretty yellow flowers. A robust plant.

Notocactus haselbergii (scarlet ball). This globe-shaped cactus is covered with soft white spines, and like most notocacti it is an excellent blooming plant that will bear flowers, unlike many cacti that will not indoors.

Opuntia basilaris (beaver tail). This group of overrated cacti never really look attractive and have a tendency to grow straggly after a time. They have blue-green pads, one growing on top of the other, and seem to belong in the desert rather than in a house. Still, because they are well-known, they are included here.

Parodia. These small but pretty cacti should be in everyone's house. They are charming and bloom indoors; the flowers are pretty and well worth the space the plant takes. They are a nice touch of color year-round. Species include *P. aureispina* (Tom Thumb cactus) and *P. sanguiniflora*.

Rebutia minuscula (red crown cactus). This small, globe-shaped plant has brilliant red flowers about 2 inches across. Such beauty is worth everyone's attention, and rebutias grow easily indoors.

Succulents   Succulents are plants with fleshy leaves and, like cacti, can store water in case you forget them. And even though most succulents need good light, there are many that make fine indoor plants if light is scanty. Because there are so many succulent plants (they appear in many plant families), it is impossible to give specific instructions for care, but some general information on how to keep them healthy is included here.

Use the same soil mix you use for cacti, and keep plants in small pots. Many succulents, like agaves and crassulas, seem to grow better when they are somewhat potbound.

Good bright light will bring better color and growth to succulents, but many can fare well even in shade. However, unlike cacti, which may bloom in shady places, most succulents in shade will not produce flowers, so be content with the lovely foliage.

Water plants somewhat heavily in summer, but keep soil just evenly moist the rest of the year. With some succulents (depending on the genus), you will have to give plants a rest in winter and keep soil just barely moist and at lower temperatures (10 degrees lower) than during the growing season. Again, as in cactus culture, use tepid water for plants, and try not to get too much water on foliage or the plants will be stained. If plants are showing new growth (generally in spring or fall), give them adequate water, but otherwise keep them on the dry side.

You can feed succulents somewhat more than cacti. In spring and summer use a 10-10-5 plant food once a month, but not at all the rest of the year. Remember that plants in shady places simply cannot assimilate plant food as readily as those in sunny places, so feed accordingly.

Try the following succulents:

Agave victoriae reginae. Want to be the envy of the neighborhood? Grow this agave; it is an impressive plant, with narrow olive-green leaves in a compact rosette. It looks more like a sculpture than a plant, and at $5 or $10 a plant it serves its purpose well. Do not get water on its leaves or

A very attractive shelf garden at windows along a stairway always provides excellent color and cheer. This is a very fine way to make bare areas into greeneries. Total construction consists of two homemade shelves. (Photo by Roche.)

water it too much because it likes a somewhat dry existence throughout its life. My plant finally grew so big across that I took it from its 10-inch pot and planted it outdoors, which was not a wise decision because although our California temperatures are not supposed to drop below 40° F, they did. After two nights at 31 degrees, the agave was mush!

Aloe nobilis. This is a rather ugly plant, but it is easy to grow in dim light. My main complaint about aloes is that their clustered rosette growth is never symmetrical or overly attractive. Otherwise aloes are amenable plants that can withstand abuse.

Crassula argentea (jade plant). Here is my candidate for a plant that can take darkness and still be beautiful. It has succulent bright green round leaves edged in red, and mature species with their branching habit are impressive "trees" at home.

Euphorbia splendens (crown of thorns). A branching plant with tiny dark green leaves and thorny branches. With some clipping and trimming, the crown of thorns becomes a thing of beauty.

E. obesa (basketball plant). As different as day from night, this plant hardly resembles most euphorbias. It is a richly colored, rounded, ridged ball. More of a curiosity than a plant, the basketball plant offers good color and is so easy to grow, even in dimly lighted areas, that it has my recommendation. Do not expect miracles from it though; it grows slowly.

Kalanchoe blossfeldiana. This is a superb flowering plant, with tiny red or orange blooms, and deserves indoor space from any garden lover. The clustering dark green leaves are handsome, and if you cut off the first batch of faded flowers in winter, you will be rewarded with another crop in spring.

Sedum. A large group of some good, some bad plants, most with small succulent round leaves. The favorite perhaps is *S. morganianum* (burro's tail) which requires basket growing. But do try some other sedums; most thrive indoors with little light.

Other Plants

Herbs can be grown in small pots at windows and furnish seasoning for cooking, far less costly than buying packaged ones. Sweet basil, chives, tarragon, rosemary, and thyme are usually easily grown in any bright window. Give them rich soil and plenty of water to make your own small herb garden. (There are several good books on herbs if you really want to get into them.)

In addition to the plants already mentioned, there are dozens of other fine window plants to grow, and in the following list we cover many of them. (Big plants like dracaenas and dieffenbachias for skylight and loft gardens are in Chapter 6.)

More Window Garden Plants

Plant	Size*	Time of Bloom	Suitable for Hanging	Window Exposure†	Remarks
Aechmea angustifolia	M	Feb.–May		W	Blue berries
A. calyculata	M	Nov.–Mar.		W	Pot offshoots when 3 inches high
Agapanthus africanus	M	July–Sept.		E	Keep potbound
A. intermedius	M	July–Sept.		E	Keep potbound
A. orientalis	M	July–Sept.		E	Keep potbound
Aglaonema commutatum	M	Dec.		N	Avoid repotting; top dress
Allamanda cathartica hendersonii	L	Aug.–Oct.	yes	S	Prune in spring
A. nerifolia	M	June–Sept.	yes	S	From Brazil
Allium neapalitanum	L	Jan.		W	Novelty; grows from bulb
Allophyton mexicanum	S	Sept.	yes	E	Worth a try
Alstroemeria pulchella	M	June		W	Rest somewhat in winter
Anthurium scherzerianum	S	Jan.–Apr.		N	Grow warm with humidity
Aphelandra aurantiaca roezlii	S	June		W	Needs good air circulation
A. chamissoniana	S	Apr.–May		W	Needs good air circulation
Ardisia crenata	M	Dec.		E	Grow cool
Arthropodium cirrhatum	M	Feb.		S	Grow cool, with humidity
Asparagus sprengeri	L	Jan.	yes	N	Spray foliage with water frequently

*Size: S (small), to 24 inches; M (medium), 24 to 36 inches; L (large), 36 inches and over.

†Window Exposure: East, E; West, W; South, S; North, N.

PLANT	SIZE	TIME OF BLOOM	SUITABLE FOR HANGING	WINDOW EXPOSURE	REMARKS
Begonia 'Alleryi'	S	Nov.–Mar.	yes	W	Easy to grow
B. coccinea	S	Mar.–June	yes	W	Angel-wing type
Beloperone guttata	M	Oct.–Nov.	yes	W	Prune in spring
Billbergia nutans	L	Jan.		E	Grow as specimen
Browallia speciosa major	M	July–Sept.		E	Grow from seed yearly
Calanthe vestita	S	Nov.–Feb.		W	Dry out severely in November
Calceolaria	S	Mar.		W	Temporary house plant
Campanula isophylla	S	Sept.	yes	E	Large flowers
C. elatines v. alba plena	M	June–Sept.	yes	E	Double white flowers
C. fragilis	S	June–Sept.	yes	E	Another good Campanula
Capsicum annuum	S	Nov.		E	The pepper plant
Chlorophytum elatum	L	Jan.	yes	W	Stands abuse
Chrysanthemum	M	Sept.–Oct.		S	Gift plant
Clerodendrum bungei	L	June–Sept.	yes	S	Somewhat difficult
C. fragrans	L	June–Sept.		S	Fragrant
Clivia miniata	L	Apr.		N	Grow quite dry for bloom
Coelogyne cristata	S	Feb.		N	Grow cool in November
C. ochracea	S	July–Aug.		E	Dry out in April
Costus igneus	S	July–Aug.		W	A real beauty
Crassula triebnerii	S	May		E	Best in winter

Plant	Size	Time of Bloom	Suitable for Hanging	Window Exposure	Remarks
Crossandra infundifuliformis	M	Apr.–Aug.		W	Requires good air circulation
Cyanotis somaliensis	S	May		W	Fine house plant
Dendrobium densiflorum	L	May		E	Fine house orchid
D. pierardii	S	Apr.–May	yes	E	Dry out in February
Dipladenia amoena	M	June	yes	S	Short rest after flowering
Epidendrum stamfordianum	M	Mar.		S	Severe rest after flowering
Eucharis grandiflora	M	Apr.		W	Watch for mealybugs
Eucomis punctata (comosa)	M	July–Aug.		E	Grows from bulb
Euphorbia pulcherrima	L	Dec.–Jan.		W	The Christmas poinsettia
E. splendens	S	Feb.–Apr.		W	Grow on the dry side
Gardenia jasminoides	M	Nov.		W	Exacting
Hibiscus rosa-sinensis	L	Nov.		S	Fine patio plant
Impatiens sultanii	S	July–Aug.		E	Everblooming in summer
Ixora coccinea	M	Mar.–July		S	Starts blooming when young
I. chinensis	M	Mar.–July		S	Brilliant red
Kaempferia roscoeana	S	June		W	A flower a day in summer
Kohleria bogotensis	M	July		E	Warmth and humidity
Mammillaria hananiana	S	Dec.		S	Good cactus

Plant	Size	Time of Bloom	Suitable for Hanging	Window Exposure	Remarks
Manettia bicolor	S	Jan.–Mar.		E	Keep potbound
Medinilla magnifica	L	Jan.	yes	W	Only mature plants bloom
Musa nana	L	Mar.		E	Pot up off-shoots
M. velutina	L	Mar.		E	Dwarf species
Oxalis cernua	S	Feb.–May	yes	S	Superior flowering plant
O. hirta	S	Jan.	yes	S	Superior flowering plant
Pelargonium	S/M	Various		W	Geranium, fine house plant
Punica granatum nana	S	Oct.		E	Good year-round plant
Rechsteineria leucotricha	S	July–Aug.		W	Rest after flowering
Rhipsalis burchelli	M	Jan.		N	Humidity and warmth
Rivina humilis	S	Sept.		E	High humidity
Rosa chinensis v. minima	S	May–Sept.		S	Cute miniature
Ruellia macrantha	M	Nov.–Jan.	yes	W	Bushy
R. makoyana	S	Nov.–Jan.	yes	W	Grow somewhat dry
Smithiantha cinnabarina	M	Nov.		E	Store tubers when dormant
S. zebrina	L	Aug.–Nov.		E	Willing bloomer
Solanum pseudocapsicum	S	Dec.		W	Temporary house plant
Sprekelia formosissima	M	Apr.		E	Grow crowded
Strelitzia reginae	L	Sept.–Oct.		S	Give poor soil

PLANT	SIZE	TIME OF BLOOM	SUITABLE FOR HANGING	WINDOW EXPOSURE	REMARKS
Streptocarpus rexii	M	Apr.–July		W	Water carefully in winter
Thunbergia erecta	M	July		S	Erect shrub
Vriesea splendens	S	June–Aug.		W	The flaming sword
Zygocactus truncatus (*Schlumbergera*)	M	Jan.–Feb.	yes	W	Dry out in November and give sun
Z. 'Gertrude Beahm'	M	Jan.–Feb.	yes	W	Dry out in November and give sun

4. Rooftop Gardens

ROOFTOP GARAGE GARDEN

If you live in a city where space is limited and long for a garden, look upward. You can have a lovely greenery on house, apartment, or garage roof. These will not be the fancy penthouse gardens you see in magazines, but your rooftop garden can be a delightful verdant scene tucked between concrete and brick buildings. When properly planned, a city rooftop garden becomes a lovely retreat. But before you start climbing to your dream garden, and before you take trowel and plants in hand, know what you are doing. Rooftop gardening involves different rules from those used for gardening on the ground. Different design attitudes are necessary too, as well as selection of the right plants.

Practical Requirements

When you start your elevated garden, consider the practical requirements. Can the roof support the weight of the soil and plants? Are there drainage facilities so excess water can escape rather than standing and thus ruining the roof and ceiling below? Is there a nearby water outlet? You do not want to lug buckets of water upstairs for plants, and in rooftop gardening plants need plenty of water. Is the flooring suitable? You can use what is there, but rarely is it attractive. Consider other types of flooring, including the loose fill materials (discussed in the flooring section).

Generally, roofs can take the extra weight of a garden and are built so water drains off freely. Still, check with the building owner to be sure of your roof's strength. If the roof has to be strengthened, the owner may help share some of the expense because a rooftop garden will increase the property value. Be sure any cracks or leaks in the present roof are repaired (this is not costly). And if drainage is anything but perfect, connect drain tiles to outlets. (There are more specifics about drainage later in the chapter.) You will want the rooftop garden to be an entity in itself, so put up fencing or railings for safety and for defining the space.

If you just dump a load of soil on a roof, you will have a mess. Use wooden planters, raised beds, or ornamental pots and tubs to hold soil

ROOFTOP GARAGE GARDEN

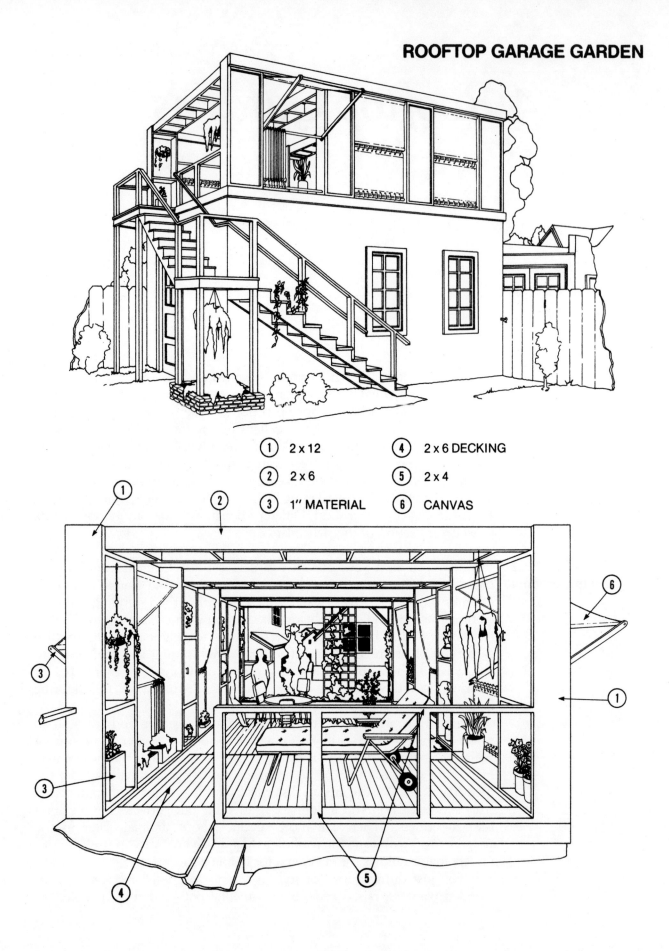

①	2 x 12	④	2 x 6 DECKING
②	2 x 6	⑤	2 x 4
③	1" MATERIAL	⑥	CANVAS

ROOFTOP GARAGE GARDEN

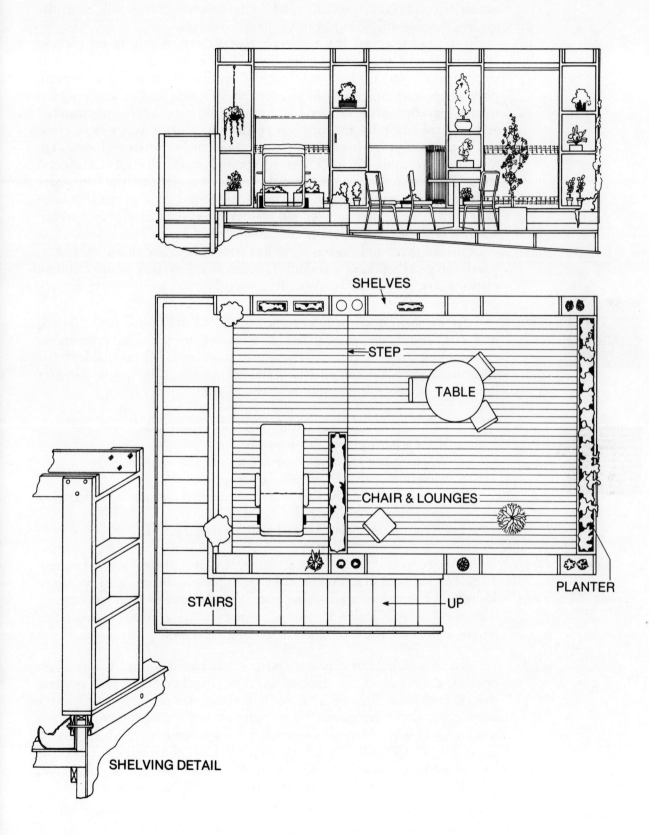

SHELVES

STEP

TABLE

CHAIR & LOUNGES

PLANTER

STAIRS

UP

SHELVING DETAIL

and plants (see Chapter 2). Use wooden dollies under containers so you can move containers after planting or so you can take plants indoors in winter. If you do not use dollies, fill containers where they will be in the garden; moving soil-filled planters is hardly a delight.

Do not tackle a vast space at once. Instead, try to plan boxes for just one corner, and then work from there. Use redwood planter boxes at various levels rather than only on the ground to establish a pattern, provide eye interest, and make tending plants much easier. Also use tubs to establish contrasting shapes. Use trellises (redwood lathing is stunning) and unusual fence designs for both beauty and a place for vines to grow.

Use the best possible soil you can get. Standard outdoor soil mixes are fine; they are available in 50- or 100-pound sacks. Recruit some good strong backs to help you get the sacks to the roof. Prepare the containers with ample drainage material; use gravel or broken pot pieces. For large tubs over 16 inches in diameter and planter boxes over 12 x 28 inches, use a 2-inch layer of gravel. Smaller containers need a 1-inch bed.

Consider the wind and sun. Wind increases evaporation in plants, which can rapidly desiccate and injure soft young leaves. And sun can bake plants. Make sure you install suitable wind barriers and shading devices.

Flooring

As we mentioned, it is possible to use the existing flooring on the roof (tar, gravel, or wood), but it is better to install a permanent, good-looking type of paving. There are many materials available; what you use depends on the specific roof and its size. When you consider flooring or paving, ask yourself these six questions:

1. *Will the paving be able to withstand weather and wear?*
2. *Will the paving be easy to maintain?*
3. *Will the paving be comfortable to walk on?*
4. *Will water drain readily from the paving?*
5. *Should the paving be light or dark in color? (Light paving creates glare; dark paving stores heat.)*
6. *What will the paving cost and how can it be installed?*

Concrete Block

Thin concrete blocks (pavers) are either smooth or rough textured. These blocks come in a concrete color or in pastels and range in size up to 16 inches. The pavers are easy to install, can be laid in sand, and can be rearranged if you make a mistake. However, water readily penetrates pavers, so be sure you have good drainage on the roof.

Tile

Tile is an ideal but expensive paving material. It is available in rough or glazed textures and two thicknesses: ¾ or ⅞ inches, and several designs, shapes, and sizes. Because it is so handsome, tile can be used almost anyplace; it is the decorator's choice whenever the roof garden adjoins a room of a house. Most tile is installed on a mortar base, which gives a finished look. Occasionally I have seen tile laid on a sand base, but the base is not permanent and always shifts. If you are going to invest in tile, let a professional install it; in the long run you will save money.

ROOFTOP GARDEN

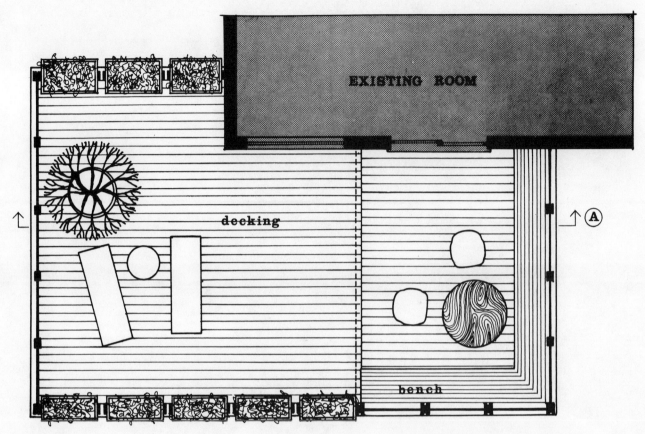

EXISTING ROOM

decking

bench

PLAN

note: the new structure is supported on existing bearing walls

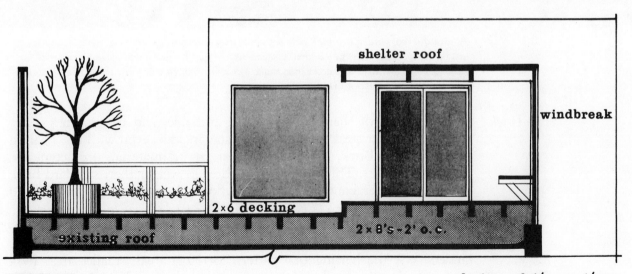

shelter roof

windbreak

2×6 decking

2 × 8's - 2' o.c.

existing roof

SECTION A

design: adrián martínez

A beautiful roof garden was built here with only the addition of a three-sided trellis. It provides just the right accent to define the area. Cyclamens, chrysanthemums, and gloxinias are used for seasonal color, and urns and accessories make this a fine roof garden. (Photo by Max Eckert; Wilds and Canon Roof Garden.)

Brick   All kinds of shapes of brick are available, and because bricks are small, they never steal the show. They stay in scale, even with the smallest foliage display. Brick, the most popular paving material, now comes in many thicknesses. Thinner brick is lighter in weight than standard brick and is thus preferable for a roof garden floor. Use rough or smooth, glazed or unglazed brick.

Brick can be laid in a great variety of patterns—herringbone, basketweave, running bond, and so on—or combined with squares of grass or cinders. Use the herringbone pattern for large areas; smaller areas look best with the running bond or basketweave designs. You can also break the large area by fitting bricks into redwood or cedar grid patterns.

Brick work requires the services of a professional mason and should be laid on a mortar base. Properly installed brick is one of the best floors.

Loosefill Materials

Loose materials such as pea gravel, cinders, fir bark, wood chips, or lavarock are inexpensive and easy to put in place. But do not expect any of these materials to be permanent; periodically they must be replaced. Use wooden strips or borders of bricks around the materials so they do not wash away in a rain. To install a gravel or pebble floor, use about 6 inches of the material to cover the roof.

Drainage

Any rooftop garden worth its weight (and weight is a factor) must have a watertight roof. Usually there is an existing layer of tar and gravel or asphalt, but to prepare the rooftop garden it is best to have a new coat of asphalt applied to really seal the roof so no water leaks through. This is not an expensive procedure and can be done easily by professional roofers. Any type of flooring can be put on the asphalt.

Once the rooftop is sealed, make sure water drains freely from the area. Drain tiles in a gravel base are an easy answer; the tiles should lead to the areas where normal gutter water is channeled. They should *not* exit on top of other people's property. Drain tiles are easy to install in a gravel base. Lay tiles around the perimeter of the specified garden area.

If existing gutters are in place, drain tiles may seem superfluous, but it is an added guarantee that water will drain off the roof and not into it, which could cause leaks and cracks to ceilings below.

This roof area is hardly large and yet a nice garden has been made using pot plants; it provides a pleasant place to relax during the day. (Photo by Matthew Barr.)

Wind and Sun   Wind and sun are the two elements that can be a blessing or a curse to your rooftop plants. When properly channeled, wind can create the good air circulation that plants need, but wind left unloosed can ruin a garden. Thus you need sturdy screens and buffers. These are generally made of wood and in interesting designs; they will enhance the garden rather than detract from it. Determine from what direction most storms and wind come from, and then install your screen or wall. But do not entirely enclose the garden or you will make your garden an enclosed prison and ruin any scenery that might add charm to the entire picture.

There are dozens of wind buffers you can make. The grid type is perhaps the best because it allows some air to circulate within the garden but blocks strong gusts.

Plants on roofs get the brunt of the noonday sun, and this sun is not good for plants. It is too intense and can burn delicate foliage and flowering plants. Even if there is ample water, excessive noonday sun can really ruin a garden quickly. So use interesting arbors and trellises to block out the sun to some extent but still allow some light to enter. A simple lath design—boards spaced apart on posts—will do the job, but the trellis or arbor is charming and will enhance the beauty of the scene.

If building or zoning laws do not allow trellises or arbors, consider canvas canopies or awnings. Use elaborate or simple designs both to shield plants from sun and to get privacy if there are neighbors above.

While many roof gardens are ornamental, this one is strictly for function: growing vegetables and beans and tomatoes in homemade planter boxes. The area is only 5 feet by 10 feet and yet produces a bountiful vegetable crop each year, enough to feed a family of four. (Photo by Gamma Photo.)

Roof gardens need not be elaborate but they can still be charming as shown in this quaint garden. The construction was minimal: a planter box and some posts with a lath ceiling—a lovely place to sit and relax. (Photo by Matthew Barr.)

Planning the Garden

Trees

Trees are the backbone of any garden, including the rooftop site. On the rooftop, only a few trees are necessary. One medium-sized accent tree and two or three smaller trees will balance the scene and provide scale.

Flowering trees, generally naturally small, are ideal for rooftop gardens. Compact and colorful, flowering trees provide great beauty, and with minimum care they grow well, even in adverse city conditions. The flowering dogwood (*Cornus florida*) is always a good choice, as is the English hawthorn (crataegus), with white flowers and red berries. The fringe tree (chionanthus) seldom grows more than 25 feet high and is full of white flowers in spring. The sourwood (*Oxydendrum arboreum*) and some of the locusts (robinas) are other fine selections. The Japanese maple (*Acer palmatum*) is another beauty that does exceedingly well in a tub. And do not forget small magnolias.

Acacia baileyana is a fine evergreen loaded with flowers in spring and rarely grows more than 20 feet when confined to a container. The camphor tree (*Cinnamomum camphora*) has a handsome branching habit,

The small roof deck garden is entered from the living room through wooden casement doors; a nice scene from both inside and out. (Photo by Matthew Barr.)

and loquats (*Eriobotrya japonica*) and all kinds of eucalyptus trees are equally fine choices. The yew pine (*Podocarpus macrophylla*) is a favorite with many people and grows almost untended. Varieties of taxus are also excellent. (There is a full list of deciduous and evergreen trees at the end of this section.)

Shrubs
Once you have selected the trees, you will need some shrubs for contrast and balance. Rhododendrons (including azaleas) are the most useful group. There are hundreds available. Rhododendrons are spectacular in bloom, yet they are just as attractive without flowers. Most will succeed in city rooftop gardens where there is some shade. All rhododendrons must be well watered in summer because they suffer more than

most plants if soil dries out. Camellias too offer a wealth of beauty for the shady rooftop that has screens or overhangs. The Japanese holly *(Ilex crenata)*, although not as showy as rhododendrons or camellias, is a reliable performer that tolerates soot and wind and still has fine green color. Japanese andromeda *(Pieris japonica)* is another good choice because it has handsome clusters of white flowers and does very well in various conditions. Roses and pyracanthas are always sure to please. (More shrubs are listed after the charts of trees.)

Using Trees and Shrubs

Select small shrubs, to 10 feet, and trees to 15 feet. Both trees and shrubs should be of varied leaf shape and pattern. On the roof, plants are surrounded by empty space or buildings. So use bold and contrasting plants to create an intimate effect.

Select plants for shape: vertical as well as horizontal, branching as well as round. Grow branching trees in tubs, round-headed shrubs in pots. Always avoid tall-growing, weak-limbed trees, because wind can be severe at times; instead, use small trees with sculpturesque growth habits, like weeping willows and crab apple. Magnolia and gray birch are good because they grow in small space and have a handsome upright pattern. Never use a single shrub; mass three or four of a kind and then repeat this arrangement elsewhere in the garden to provide balance.

Use mulches—peat moss, fir bark—over the soil to prevent rapid dryout and help keep roots cool and moist. Feed plants every other watering with a 10-10-5 plant food. Do water plants copiously; because they are exposed to direct sun and wind, plants dry out quickly. In fact, trees and shrubs will need water every other day.

Deciduous Trees

BOTANICAL AND COMMON NAME	HEIGHT, IN FEET (APPROXIMATE)	REMARKS
Acer palmatum (Japanese maple)	20	Needs rich, well-drained soil
Albizzia julibrissin (silk tree)	20	Very ornamental
Betula populifolia (gray birch)	40	Yellow color in autumn
Cornus florida (dogwood)	25	A stellar ornamental
Crataegus mollis (downy hawthorn)	30	Pear-shaped red fruit
C. oxyacantha (English hawthorn)	20	Pink to red flowers

Gingko biloba (maidenhair tree)	60	Popular
Laburnum watereri (golden chain tree)	25	Deep yellow flowers
Magnolia stellata (star magnolia)	20	Very ornamental
Malus baccata (Siberian crab apple)	45	Lovely flowers and fruit
M. floribunda (Japanese flowering crab apple)	30	Handsome foliage and flowers
Robinia pseudoacacia	60	Fine, late spring flowers
Salix babylonica (weeping willow)	40	Fast grower
Sorbus aucuparia	45	Red autumn color

Evergreen Trees

BOTANICAL AND COMMON NAME	HEIGHT, IN FEET (APPROXIMATE)	REMARKS
Acacia baileyana (Bailey acacia)	20–30	Profuse yellow flowers
Bauhinia blakeana (orchid tree)	20	Abundant flowers; partially deciduous
Cinnamomum camphora (camphor tree)	40	Dense branching habit
Eriobotrya japonica (loquat)	20	Needs well-drained soil
Eucalyptus gunnii (cider gum)	20–75	Shade or screen tree
Picea abies (excelsa) (Norway spruce)	75	Not for small areas
Podocarpus macrophylla (yew pine)	60	Grows untended
Taxus cuspidata 'Capitata' (Japanese yew)	50	Good sturdy tree

Shrubs

Botanical and Common Name	Height, in Feet (approximate)	Remarks
Abelia grandiflora (glossy abelia)	5	Free flowering
Chaenomeles speciosa (flowering quince)	6	Lovely flowers
Euonymus alatus (winged euonymus)	9	Sturdy; easily grown
E. japonica (evergreen euonymus)	15	Splendid foliage
Forsythia intermedia (border forsythia)	2-9	Deep yellow flowers
F. ovata (early forsythia)	8	Earliest to bloom and hardiest
Ilex cornuta (Chinese holly)	9	Bright berries; lustrous foliage
Ligustrum amurense (Amur privet)	6-30	Small spikes of white flowers
Photinia serrulata (Chinese photinia)	36	Bright red berries
Pieris japonica (Japanese andromeda)	9	Splendid color
Pyracantha coccinea (scarlet firethorn)	8-10	Many varieties; valued for bright berries
Rhododendron	8-15	Lovely flowers; evergreen leaves
Rosa (rose)	8-15	Many fine varieties
Salix caprea (French pussy willow)	25	Vigorous grower

Vegetables   There are many vegetables you can grow on the rooftop garden, but do not tackle too much too soon. Vegetables do require care: watering every other day or every day (depending on rainfall), protection against insects, thinning (most of them), and so forth.

For a start, grow some carrots, beets, tomatoes, cucumbers, and lettuce. Since most, if not all, your vegetables will be grown in planters, avoid the space-taking crops like cauliflower, cabbage, and corn. You will be doing an injustice to the plants and yourself if you try to grow them.

You can start vegetable seeds indoors and then transplant them outside when weather is warm. You can also use prestarted plants. These plants have passed the crucial stage of germination and are already up and growing. All that prestarts require are transplanting into rich soil in planters and then routine care.

Grow vegetables fast, that is, with plenty of water; you want lush growth to produce a good harvest. Use a vegetable plant food every other watering once plants are started and 6 to 10 inches tall. Remember that vegetables last only a season rather than for years. A list of the best vegetables for your rooftop garden follows, with seed time, growing time, and so on.

Vegetable	Planting Time for Seed or Prestarts	Seed Depth, Inches	Growing Days	Comments
Beets	seed 3 weeks before last frost	½	60	generally an easy crop not bothered by insects
Carrots	seed 2 weeks before last frost	¼	75	lots of carrots for little effort
Eggplant	transplant prestarts after last frost		70	better than you think
Lettuce (leaf)	seed 4 weeks before last frost	¼	45	use thinnings for salads
Lettuce (butterhead)	seed 4 weeks before last frost	¼	75	handled like head lettuce; small, delicious
Lettuce (head)	seed 3 weeks before last frost	¼	85	stands heat better than other types
Peppers	transplant prestarts after last frost		70	start seeds indoors or buy prestarts

Radishes	seed 4 weeks before last frost	¼	25	the easiest to grow
Spinach	seed 3 weeks before last frost	½	48	does not like hot weather
Squash	seed after last frost	1	summer types: 55 winter types: 100	bush or vine type are heavy producers
Tomatoes	transplant prestarts after last frost		70	need care but worth it

Vines   Vines cover a multitude of sins—unsightly walls, awkward corners—and flowering vines are majestic in bloom. Vines are also excellent for fences and screens because they become living tapestries and thus enhance the rooftop area. Most vines grow fast, can take sun or wind, and need only trimming and staking to perform at their best. Also, once established, vines provide privacy and are the finishing touch to a fine rooftop greenery. Here are some ideal vines:

Akebia quinata (five-leaf akebia). Vigorous twiner; fragrant small flowers. Sun or partial shade.

Ampelopsis brevipedunculata (blueberry climber). Strong grower with dense leaves. Sun or shade.

Aristolochia durior (Dutchman's pipe). Big twiner with mammoth leaves. Sun or shade.

Clematis armandii (evergreen clematis). Lovely flowers and foliage. Sun.

Euonymus fortunei (winter creeper). Shiny, leathery leaves; orange berries in fall. Sun or shade.

Hedera helix (English ivy). Scalloped neat leaves; many varieties. Shade.

Hydrangea petiolaris (climbing hydrangea). Heads of snowy flowers. Sun or partial shade.

Ipomoea purpurea (morning glory). White, blue, purple, pink, or red flowers. Sun.

Lonicera japonica halliana (Hall's honeysuckle). Deep green leaves that turn bronze in fall. Sun or shade.

A *vegetable garden in the sky in a tiny space* is a delight to the eye and the palate. (Photo by Gamma Photo.)

Parthenocissus quinquefolia (Virginia creeper). Scarlet leaves in fall. Sun or shade.

Pueraria thunbergiana (kudzu vine). Purple flowers. Sun or partial shade.

Rosa (rambler rose). Many varieties. Sun.

Vitis coignetiae (glory grape). Colorful autumn leaves. Sun or partial shade.

Wisteria floribunda (Japanese wisteria). Violet-blue flowers. Sun.

Annuals and Perennials

You can grow almost any kind of annual (last only a season) or perennial (bloom year after year) in your rooftop garden. Grow masses of one kind of plant for a real display. If you keep annuals and perennials well watered and in good sun, you will have a bounty of flowers. Put plants in 8- to 12-inch-deep redwood boxes.

Plants are available at nurseries at seasonal times ready for planting; select what you like because there is no limitation. On roofs there is ample sun, which is the prerequisite for most flowers. Stake tall growers so wind does not break stems. For specific annuals and perennials, select from those described in the next chapter.

5. Balcony, Porch, and Modular Gardens

Balconies Many apartments now have balconies. These areas can, with some alteration, become beautiful gardens, gardens that will alleviate the confines of a city. Unfortunately, many people do not take advantage of a small balcony; they just dump a few plants on the balcony and let things go at that. A much more beneficial attitude is to consider the small balcony as a garden and plan it accordingly, taking your time and choosing proper containers and plants.

Balconies are being made larger than they were years ago, so the average person definitely can have a garden without any land. This chapter will get you started on making that outdoor space into a beautiful indoor-outdoor garden.

Balcony Basics There are a few basic facts you should know about balcony gardens before you start, some good, some bad. First, let us consider the good things. Most balconies are already on the property and require just a little alteration. Generally, balconies are large enough to create a pleasant greenery. Also, balconies can easily become indoor-outdoor gardens, since they are visible from the inside—the garden makes a lovely scene. Finally, garden balconies will lift your spirits immeasurably.

Now the bad things about balcony gardens. Wind will always be a problem, so you have to either protect plants from the strong gales that can harm them or grow plants that will not be hurt by winds. On the average balcony, light can be a problem because generally there is a balcony above you. Thus, you must carefully select plants.

Obviously the advantages outweigh the disadvantages, so balcony gardening does make sense. Just make sure you approach the garden with an intelligent eye. Begin with a sketch of the balcony area. This will give you the shape and size as a starting point to work from. Once you have done the rough sketch, start penciling in shapes of planters to determine whether square or rectangular boxes will do or whether pots and tubs will suit the area better. Make a lot of sketches until you have a balanced

BALCONY GARDEN

landscape plan where there is mass, line, and vertical as well as horizontal dimension. This will give you a total balcony composition rather than a spotty-looking garden.

Typical Balcony Arrangements

Balconies may be long and narrow, L-shaped, or nearly square. The long and narrow balcony is the type most often found in high-rise apartments. This balcony is short of space, so to add more growing area, consider vertical panels of trellises at each end of the balcony to act as both wind buffers and places for plants. The floor area is usually only 6 to 8 feet, so do not use too many pot plants on the floor level; use the balcony ledge. If the ledge is narrow, extend it with a wooden platform. In any case, whenever there are pots on a balcony ledge, you must have a railing—it is an essential part of safety. The wood or iron railing can be decorative to add beauty to the balcony.

Use vining plants on the side panels of the trellises and trailing plants on the ledges. For floor plants, group small pots, but elevate them on platforms. Lifting the garden off the ground will make it look like more than it is; several pots of plants at different heights will add dimension and scale to the small balcony.

The L-shaped balcony has more floor space than the long narrow one. On this balcony you can use some terraced planters in one corner as eye interest. Use a mass of plants at different levels. Balance this setting with a vertical accent adjacent to the corner level; fill in between with smaller pot plants or a long stone or masonry planter to create a marriage between one area of the plant material and the other.

If you decide on some screening for the L-shaped balcony, use narrow panels so you do not shut off the view. Use the screening only on one end; leave the other end open. Set a pair of treelike plants on each side of the doorway to the balcony, and do the same on the inside of the doorway. This arrangement (a favorite decorator's trick) melds indoors with outdoors, creating a unique transition.

The square balcony has more space than the other two types but ironically presents a more complex landscaping problem. Here it is difficult to create a center of interest because of the monotony of the space, so use round tubs at one end to bring circles into the square design. Use several tubs of different heights (but of the same motif) in a corner so there is a mass of green. In another corner place one stellar tree in an ornamental pot to balance the scene. Now that you have the center of interest and the counter interest, bring the garden together by using low masses of plants stretching from one area to another. These may be small pots in a row or, better yet, a stone planter filled with low-growing shrubs and such. A trellis at one end will add vertical dimension and extend the garden area physically and visually.

Porches

We considered new buildings with balconies, but old buildings and flats have porches that can be turned into green Edens. I spent my childhood in a flat. The building had a back porch, and after observing years of nothingness out there, I decided to convert the large porch area

BALCONY TRELLIS

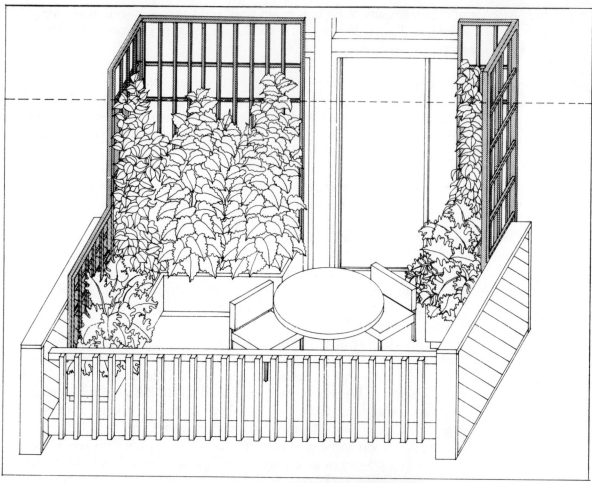

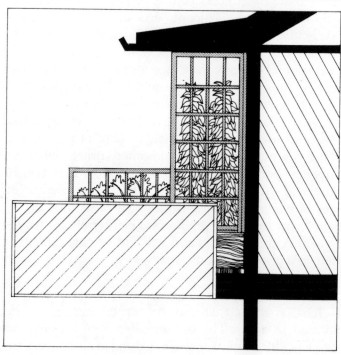

**side
elevation**

PORCH GARDEN

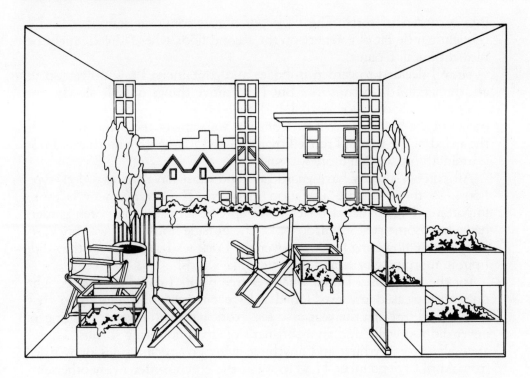

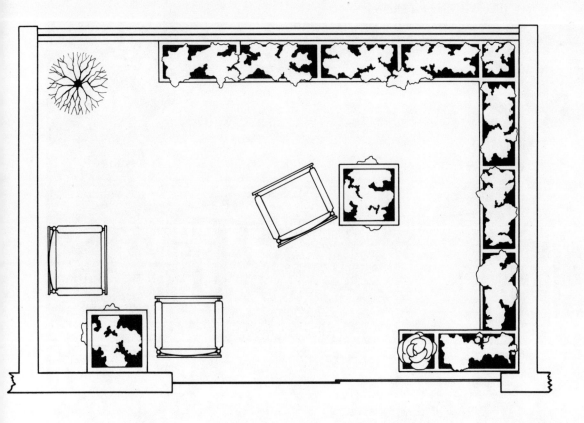

into a garden of sorts. The back porch had common stairways, and I thought a little bit of greenery on the second floor, where I lived, might be pleasant for all tenants.

Since I decided to garden in boxes and containers, I saw no reason to ask the landlord's permission. But I did move things outside slowly, not in one big swoop. Not until I had a dozen plants in big tubs did the owner of the building ask if the constant watering of the plants might rot the wood of the porch. I replied that it rained frequently and that did not hurt anything, so...No more was said.

All porches already have guard rails and most have wooden deck-type floors, so there is little alteration involved. The arrangement is more important. I constructed boxes to fit specific areas so the porch garden had a handsome custom-made look. The outside house wall was brick, so I grew some flowering vines to cover the brick walls. And cover they did; I put in morning glories and they grew like weeds!

For the porch area I used whatever free plants I could get and bought ones that pleased my eye. I had a large citrus, a blue plumbago that flowered all through the year, assorted exotic gingers (however, the gingers never did too well), and an assortment of small flowering shrubs. Thus I grew almost everything and anything, with no specific rules or worries from April to September. I had to water the porch garden every other day. There was another porch above mine, thus providing a ceiling over my

What could have been a bare porch results in a flowerland with the addition of some boxes; this garden extends onto the roof of a garage to create a handsome, colorful addition to daily living. (Photo by Gamma Photo.)

garden, so rain did not hit my plants. I regularly trimmed and pruned plants. At that time, packaged plant foods were not yet on the market, so I replenished soil frequently to supply plants with a constant supply of nutrients. I bought the soil in bulk at a nursery and can still remember carrying it upstairs in bushel baskets and shopping bags.

I always thought that if the building were mine, I would glass in the porch and have a regular greenhouse porch garden. I asked the landlord about this, and that was when he put his foot down!

Thus, utilize your porch (if you have one) as I did. If you want to enclose the porch, as I wanted to, install glass windows on the sides and roofing material on the ceiling. If you live on the top floor, reroof completely and put in dome skylights (skylights are discussed in the next chapter).

Plants for the Balcony and Porch

The balcony or porch garden is generally small, about 8 by 15 feet. Large trees, even small ones (to 15 feet), are usually not for these areas because there is not enough height or floor space. You want plants that are compact yet handsome, small (to 6 feet), and really special. And because the balcony or porch garden is seasonal (no one wants to go out to garden in severe winter weather), you will want lots of color, which means many annuals and perennials, along with a few shrubs and a special small tree. Annuals and perennials are easy to grow from prestarts; simply transplant the prestarts into containers and grow them as you would other plants.

Because your plants will be in containers of various shapes and sizes, you must really plan. Try to map out the porch or balcony garden so space is used wisely; use custom-made planters made to fit specific areas (see Chapter 2). Wind and sun have to be dealt with. Water daily or every other day, and have a biweekly feeding program for the annuals and perennials.

The following list of plants (annuals and perennials) will give you an idea of what you can grow; however, if there are some plants you particularly like but they are not on the list and you want them, by all means give them a try. (Also see the trees and shrubs sections in Chapter 4.)

Annuals

Ageratum houstonianum (floss flower). Blue, white, or pink varieties. Plant is available from 4 to 22 inches tall and blooms from early summer until fall. Forms compact mounds of foliage. Needs well-drained soil and somewhat heavy watering.

Althaea rosea (hollyhock). I recommend hollyhocks because they are so colorful and survive in practically any situation. However, use them only if you have enough room because they grow to 6 feet. The large flowers are pink, rose, yellow, red, or white.

Antirrhinum majus (snapdragon). Tall, stately, and lovely annuals with beguiling flowers; there are many colors to choose from, except blue. Snapdragons come in many heights and make superb vertical accents in

A very small balcony that became a no-land garden with the addition of some pot plants. If trellises were installed on the stucco walls it could be a verdant greenery; yet even a few plants bring cheer to both indoors and out. (Photo by Matthew Barr.)

the garden. Will tolerate some shade, but basically snapdragons prefer sun. To increase bloom yield, cut flowers frequently and remove faded blossoms. Many varieties in many sizes.

Calendula officinalis (calendula, pot marigold). Bright rounded flowers in a variety of colors: orange, cream, or gold. Pot marigolds grow 12 to 24 inches tall and bloom all summer. They are hard to beat and grow with almost no care. A workhorse of the garden.

Callistephus chinensis (aster, China aster). These 1- to 3-foot plants have wiry stems and beautiful white to deep red flowers. Some are early blooming, others bloom in midseason, and still others provide late color. They are one of the best flowers for cutting.

Centaurea cyanus (bachelor's button, cornflower). Growing to a height of 2½ feet, these fine plants bear pink, white, wine, or blue flowers. Their gray-green foliage makes a dramatic display, and although they require pinching and pruning, they bloom profusely.

Coleus blumei (coleus). A foliage plant that comes in a multitude of colors. The tapestry-colored toothed leaves are an asset in any garden, and plants can reach to 3 feet or more. Pinch growing tips to make them compact. Good background plant.

Here is an example of a porch that could easily be enclosed to make a fine garden; porch construction already has all necessary components. All that is needed is some glass to really make the garden bloom. (Photo by Gamma Photo.)

Dianthus (pink, sweet William). There are so many varieties that you are apt to be confused, but do try the plants; they have clusters of pink or white flowers. Pinks are easy to grow and are available in many heights. Another workhorse of the garden.

Iberis umbellata (candytuft). Masses of flowers make candytuft a good choice for the beginning gardener. Plants mound to 12 or 15 inches, and in late spring and early summer bloom their heads off. Flower color may be pink, salmon, or white. Good for cutting or garden display.

Impatiens balsamina (impatiens). Get to know these plants because they have many virtues in the garden: they come in many different colors and heights and bloom profusely. They like some sun but also succeed in shade.

Lobularia maritima (sweet alyssum). Available in several colors, this low-growing annual has a multitude of uses when combined with other plants or used as filler around perennials. Will grow in hot, dry situations if necessary.

Phlox drummondii (phlox). These annuals, which grow to 16 inches, have lovely clusters of 1-inch flowers. Choice of color includes rose, crimson, salmon, white, scarlet, and violet, often with contrasting eyes. Bloom is abundant, and plants are seldom bothered by insects. Grow in sun with plenty of water.

Senecio cruentus (cineraria). Here is an annual that will bloom in shade. The daisylike flowers come in light or dark shades of blue, purple, and magenta. Plants grow from 12 to 15 inches and have handsome foliage. Keep them shady and moist in a well-drained place.

Tagetes erecta (marigold). These all-time favorites are the backbone of a garden. Plants grow quickly, come in all sizes from 6 to 40 inches, and bloom constantly from summer to fall. The blossoms come in many shades of yellow, orange, dark red, and maroon. Plants can be used by themselves for lovely accents or with other plantings. There are many types: the French dwarfs, to 18 inches, in a fine array of color; African dwarfs, to 16 inches; and some of the new varieties. Most types need an evenly moist soil in a sunny place.

Tropaeoleum majus (nasturtium). Underrated, nasturtiums can bring an immense wealth of color to the first garden, and easier plants to grow cannot be found. Nasturtiums bloom from early summer until frost and now come in single, semidouble, or double flowers in shades of yellow, orange, crimson, pink, maroon, and multicolored varieties. Use dwarf plants for borders, the taller varieties for spot color. Most nasturtiums will grow rapidly with little care.

A small porch garden with pot plants helps take the bare look away from this entrance. (Photo by Matthew Barr.)

Zinnia elegans (zinnia). This popular annual has great diversity. There are many sizes, forms, heights, and colors. Zinnias have infinite uses in the garden and are fast growers that need little care but plenty of moisture. Flower color includes orange, yellow, pink, red, lavender, and some bicolors.

Perennials *Alyssum saxatile* (basket of gold). Splashes of golden flowers make this a desirable garden plant. Foliage is gray and provides an interesting contrast in the garden. (Do not confuse this plant with the annual sweet alyssum, which is called Lobularia.)

Anchusa azurea (bugloss). Clusters of bright blue blossoms make this an outstanding addition in the garden. Make sure you have room though; they can grow to 6 feet. Some excellent new varieties are now available.

Aster frikartii (aster), *A. novae-angliae* (New England aster). Their dramatic blue and purple flowers make these two perennials outstanding. The daisylike flowers, which are produced in abundance, are bright and showy. Plants are available in several heights and make fine displays in large drifts. They like lots of sun and water.

Astilbe japonica (false spirea). A perennial for shady places, plant has white, pink, or red flowers on wiry stems. The bronze-green leaves are attractive; the bloom season is summer. Ideal for mixing with shrubby plants. Plant grows to about 24 inches. Moist soil is essential.

Campanula persicifolia (bellflower). These should be grown more often because they offer so much color. With their white or blue flowers in June

Basic construction elements of this porch–garage-top garden are well shown in this photo. In such an area you can grow dozens of plants. (Photo by Gamma Photo.)

and July, they form mounds of color and grow to 10 inches. Give plants full sun or light shade, and be sure they are in well-drained soil.

Chrysanthemum maximum (chrysanthemum), *Chrysanthemum morifolium* (Shasta daisy). These are available in a multitude of shapes: spoon, cushion, pompom, and button. Colors vary from white to yellow, gold, or orange. Heights are variable, and there are chrysanthemums for all kinds of uses in the garden. Will tolerate dry soils and still flourish.

Delphinium elatum (delphinium, larkspur). Handsome, tall plants, with spires of large flowers. Excellent for background plantings. Colors range from white to pink to superb blues. Rich, well-drained soil and sun are essential. *D. grandiflorum,* known as Chinese delphinium, is also handsome.

Gaillardia aristata (blanketflower). Gaillardias produce showy flowers over a long period of time. The blooms are daisylike and generally bright yellow, although bronzy scarlet types have been introduced too. Undemanding, they do best in a slightly sandy soil with adequate sun.

Gypsophila paniculata (baby's breath). Dainty, lacy plants that grow rapidly to 2 feet and bear small, rounded, white flowers in masses. (There are also pink and white varieties.) Blooms last over a month, and plants make excellent garden fillers.

Hemerocallis (daylily). These large plants have fountains of grassy foliage and yellow, cream, or bronze flowers. Plants start blooming in May and continue on and off until frost. Need sun. Note that most are tall and rangy and thus need lots of space.

Papaver orientale (Oriental poppy). These are coming into popularity again, and it is difficult to find more dramatic flowers than their bold orange blooms. Once established, they bloom profusely. Plants are 2 to 4 feet high, with 6- to 8-inch flowers. They need well-drained soil and some sun, but not direct, intense sun.

Phlox subulata (summer phlox, moss pink). Three- to 5-foot plants bear a wealth of large pink-tone flowers. Phlox are compatible with most garden flowers and make splendid accents. However, they do need a deep, fertile soil and sun to prosper.

Modular Gardens

I am often asked, "Just what is a modular garden?" It is essentially a container garden with plants in movable planters or boxes. The containers are not interlocking but they fit together like blocks or triangles to form pleasing patterns.

The modular garden is a form of garden that allows you to have the maximum of plantings in minimum space. Planters always look handsome, and you can grow anything in modular boxes, from cacti to succulents to shrubs, annuals, or perennials. Thus, you can have great flexibility in this kind of gardening.

Boxes for your modular gardens can be simple: five pieces of wood nailed or screwed together. Or the boxes can be more complex, made of rods and dowels (no nails). For uniformity, any modular box can be painted one color, left natural if redwood, or coated with a preservative if you use other than redwood.

No matter what kind of box you decide on, remember that drainage holes are essential so excess water can run off. You can plant directly into the box or use plastic liners (with holes punched in the bottom of the plastic. In a space of 5 x 10 feet, by intelligently stacking boxes you can have room for dozens of plants. If you have more space, the design can be linear, at ground level. Remember that stacked boxes are easier to tend because they are at waist level.

Modular gardens can occupy a small area of a patio or a corner of a yard, or be against a fence, on a porch, or at one end of a balcony. In any situation the modular garden offers a great deal of gardening space in minimum space.

MODULAR GARDEN

MODULAR CONTAINERS

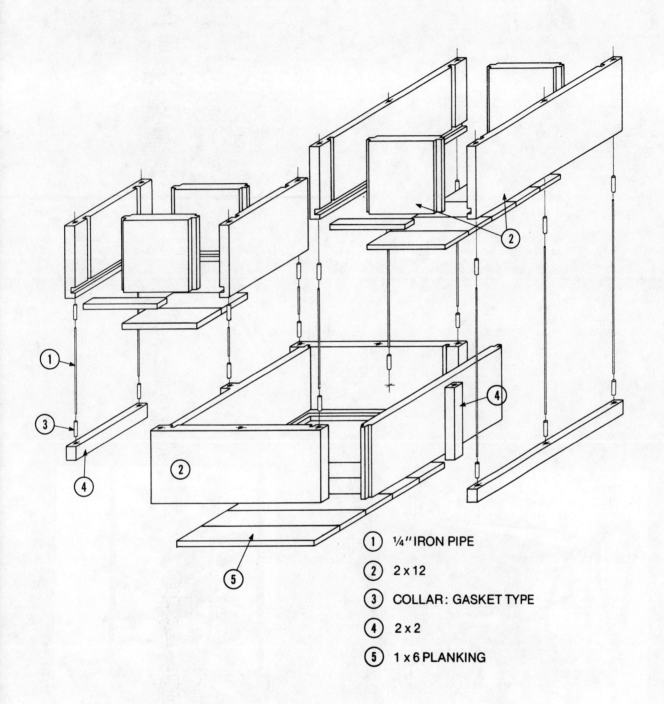

1. ¼" IRON PIPE
2. 2 x 12
3. COLLAR: GASKET TYPE
4. 2 x 2
5. 1 x 6 PLANKING

6. Skylight (Atrium) and Loft Gardens

Atriums   An atrium is an open space in the center of a house. The space is usually used as a garden. Without a roof the atrium has limited usage, but with a roof it is an all-year garden, what I call a skylight garden. Areas set aside within a house (not in the center) can also be gardens; perhaps there is a corner, nook, or length of a room where space is available. These spots too can be greeneries, with some minor construction modification. Usually the addition of skylights (perhaps floodlamps) and some planter bins can make the indoor garden even if you do not have any outdoor land.

The beauty of the skylight garden is that it creates an outdoor area indoors in almost any house situation. The mechanics are simple: a small indoor area within a room defined with partitions and domes or skylights in the ceiling. In such spaces you can grow all kinds of tropical house plants. Although the skylight garden is on a larger scale than the window garden, it becomes an integral part of the home, usually visible from several locations. The skylight garden is an indoor greenery par excellence, with natural top light for plants. (Do not confuse the skylight garden with a greenhouse or a garden room, which are separate areas for plants.)

Lofts   As you scout your house for space for indoor plants, do not forget lofts. Lofts are generally small upper balconies, usually overlooking the living room. The contractors who include them in homes had some idea for their use, but generally lofts are more an illusion of space than a usable room. Most lofts are quite small, but they can become indoor gardens. There is more construction involved than with a skylight garden, but it is not enough to deter you. In the loft garden, as in the skylight garden, you will need domes or skylights and some arrangement to at least partially enclose the area (perhaps sliding glass doors).

SKYLIGHT GARDEN

Design Adrían Martínez

Interior View

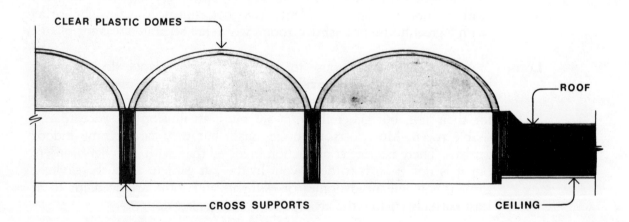

CLEAR PLASTIC DOMES

ROOF

CROSS SUPPORTS

CEILING

Detail

LOFT GARDEN

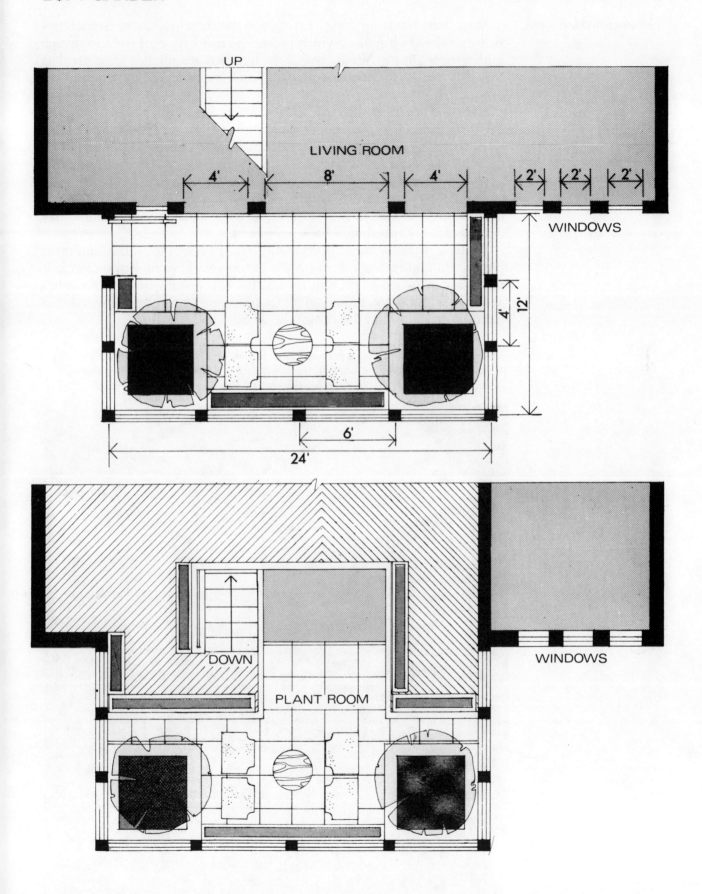

Other Considerations

Most loft areas are long and narrow, with windows or sometimes skylights already installed, which makes the conversion of the spot into a garden quite simple. What have to be installed are suitable glass dividers that will enclose the area and perhaps some more skylights for additional light.

Sliding glass doors are fine for the front of the loft. They open and close easily and allow adequate ventilation within the garden. But for a more charming effect, use wooden casement doors—those used for French doors. With some know-how you can install doors yourself; doors come in stock sizes and are available at supply houses.

The floor of the garden is important. Wood floors will be a problem because even if you have plants in suitable saucers, water stains may develop. Ideally you should have a tile floor.

Wall and window construction will already exist in lofts. But you must prevent humidity from ruining the structure. Use moisture-retardant paints and redwood to prevent rot and decay, especially in window sashes and frames. Put wood preservatives (at hardware stores) on old wood that has been stripped, and then paint the wood.

This magnificent schefflera lives a fine life under a skylight and furnishes needed mass and color to the area; the plant has done so well it saves the expense of drapery at the windows because it completely covers the glass. (Photo by Max Eckert.)

What You Can Grow: Planning the Garden

Because of the height, in a suitable skylight garden you can grow both large plants and smaller plants, from trees to house plants. This is the area to have your specimen plants, your palms and ferns, and perhaps some orchids. Because the area is always on display, plants always must be at their peak. Generally, you do not want too many plants, but you will want enough plants to create a green feeling. The average garden, say, 10 x 10 feet, will need about fifty plants to make it glow with color.

The main idea in the skylight or loft garden is to have a pleasing arrangement. Approach the landscape as you would an outdoor one; that is, use verticals and horizontals, mass and line. Create a total picture by using groups of plants in one area balanced by another group of plants in another area. You will need about two or three large trees in a clump to set the mood of the garden. Large schleffleras or fishtail palms are excellent choices for vertical proportion. Put them in one corner, with lower, more bushy plants like pittosporums or self-heading philodendrons in another corner to balance the scene. Arrange smaller house plants, if lush enough, in a row or in groups of three or five in three areas of the room. For maximum effect use plants of the same kind; this gives a full massive look to the garden. Ficus and dieffenbachias grow quite tall and so are well-suited to the skylight or loft garden, providing dramatic and compelling interest.

Choose containers carefully; too many of different designs can look confusing. Use ornamental but simple pots of one kind for one area of the room and then another design in another part of the room. Always be careful not to create a clash between color or motif.

If you put too many plants in the area or use too many different pots, you will create eye confusion. Keep the arrangement clean but lovely; use a restrained hand. And always leave plenty of walking space in your garden.

Here are some suitable plants for skylight and loft gardens:

Crassula (jade tree)

This large plant group includes a single plant that makes an excellent small tree: *Crassula argentea.* It has a thick trunk and glossy green succulent leaves. The jade tree does very well indoors and likes a lot of water but should not be drowned; ideally, it should be allowed to dry out between waterings. Crassula will thrive in a bright, somewhat warm place, say, 75°F.

Citrus

This group of plants can be grown indoors or outdoors. Orange, grapefruit, lime, or lemon trees are handsome additions to loft or skylight gardens, but they need good sun for most of the day. Citrus also need plenty of water in spring and summer because they have a fast flush of growth. In fall and winter plants rest somewhat, so ease up on watering and provide cooler temperatures (60°F) at night.

Most citrus will grow in any soil, but a rather dense, claylike soil is best. Fertilize the plant every other watering when it is in active growth, but not at all the rest of the year. Trim and prune to desired tree shape. There are many varieties at suppliers; try these two:

Plastic skylights furnish light for many plants in an atrium garden. The brick built-in unit and planting arrangement are attractive and accommodate many plants; even a morning glory grows up the post at left. (Photo courtesy Kentile Corp.)

Citrus ponderosa (lemon tree). Dark green oval leaves.

C. taitensis (orange tree). Small dark green foliage. Several varieties.

Schefflera (Australian umbrella tree)

They have changed the name of this plant many times, but it is usually listed under schefflera (occasionally brassaia). This is the Australian umbrella tree that can grow to 6 or 7 feet with large stately leaves in compounds.

Scheffleras like large containers and a good rich soil. They require plenty of water, but let plants dry out a bit before rewatering. Put the plant in a bright but not very sunny place. To attain the treelike look, cut off young growth as it appears at the base; eventually you will have a lovely crown of leaves at the top. There is only one species commonly offered: *Schefflera actinophylla*.

Philodendrons

There are so many philodendrons that it is important to choose carefully when selecting plants from this group. Some are quite handsome and can be trained to tree growth; others are straggly and never amount to much. Philodendrons are popular, but they are not that easy to grow because they are jungle denizens and need very humid, warm conditions, which are lacking in most homes.

A garden in a bathroom where once there was none? Why not? Here it is done with artificial lights. The foliage plants grow lushly and include ficus elastica and philodendrons. (Photo by Hedrich-Blessing.)

This jungle grows under a huge skylight at the top and furnishes a stellar green display. (Photo by Gamma Photo.)

Generally give plants an evenly moist soil, good feeding, and a bright location. Pruning, clipping, and staking are necessary to keep plants at their best. Here are some species to try:

Philodendron deliciosa (Monstera deliciosa) (Swiss-cheese plant). This plant has large leaves that are deeply lobed.

P. panduraeforme. Fiddle-shaped leaves; good color.

P. soderoi. Heart-shaped dark green leaves; lovely.

One 37-inch-square acrylic dome furnishes the light for this group of lovely plants. (Photo by Matthew Barr.)

P. squamiferum. Scalloped and shiny dark green leaves.

Palms   Any loft or indoor greenery will benefit from the addition of a palm. These graceful and elegant plants add beauty to almost any area and are surprisingly one of the easiest indoor plants to grow.

Palms come from all over the world and as a group include: howea, caryota, chamaedorea, and rhapis. Generally, palms like a moist soil and then a drying out before water is reapplied. Most palms need some sun to keep shapely and healthy; in shade palms can become spindly. Palms do very well in average home temperatures with somewhat cool nights (65°F).

Remember that most palms grow in spring and summer and rest the balance of the year, so never try to force them into growth. Here are some palms that have decorated my indoor gardens through the years:

Caryota mitis (fishtail palm). Large plant with erect trunk and canopies of dark green wedge-shaped leaves.

Chamaedorea erumpens (bamboo palm). Tall-stemmed plant with bamboo-like leaves. Takes abuse.

Howea fosteriana (sentry or kentia palm). A very popular plant; graceful and lovely. It needs shade and should be grown quite moist in spring and summer, with less moisture and cooler temperatures (65°F) in winter. Avoid feeding too much.

Rhapis excelsa (lady palm). Smaller in size than the other palms mentioned; grows to about 4 feet. This is a compact, many-stemmed plant of lush growth.

Ficus   The rubber tree (*Ficus elastica decora*), with its broad spatula-shaped leaves, has long been a favorite. The well-known fiddleleaf fig (*F. lyrata*) has very large crinkly leaves. The weeping fig or banyan tree (*F. benjamina*) has also become an indoor tree subject.

Grow ficus plants in a somewhat sandy soil kept evenly moist. Bright light suits the plants, and average home humidity and temperatures are satisfactory. Some species, notably *F. lyrata*, are notoriously averse to drafts, so be sure plants have a protected area away from doors that will be open and closed. Try the following specimens in your loft or skylight gardens:

F. benjamina (weeping fig). Dense, with pendant branches and small green leaves.

F. diversifolia (mistletoe fig). Charming, with tiny round leaves. Does not grow as tall as other ficus plants.

A built-in no-land garden with artificial light at top to furnish illumination for plants. The plants (philodendrons and ficus) are planted in soil with a covering of white gravel. (Photo courtesy General Electric Co.)

F. elastica decora (rubber tree). Oval glossy green foliage.

F. lyrata (fiddleleaf fig). Mammoth dark green textured leaves.

F. roxburghii. Large scalloped leaves, can be trained to a single trunk.

Dracaenas

This is a group of popular indoor treelike plants. Most dracaenas come from Africa, Madagascar, and other areas of the world with sharply defined seasons; that is, it rains for months and then is somewhat dry for months. Thus it is a good idea to keep these plants somewhat dry all year, but never bone dry. The most popular plant in the group is *Dracaena marginata,* which makes a beautiful indoor tree. *D. fragrans massangeana* is also handsome but needs severe pruning. To do this, occasionally trim off new growth as it starts at the bottom of the trunk and allow only a few growths at the top of the plant to mature.

Most dracaenas do fine in average room temperatures and a somewhat shady location and need little care to prosper in the loft garden. Here are some I grow:

Dracaena fragrans massangeana. Open, bright green leaves margined yellow.

D. marginata. Lance-shaped leaves, dark green and edged red.

D. werneckii. Rosette plant with green and white leaves; can grow to 8 feet.

Dieffenbachias

These large-leaved plants usually have a single trunk and multicolored foliage—yellow-and-green, white-and-green—making them splendid accent plants. They grow easily in the home but do not attain treelike qualities until they are about 6 years old.

From Central America or Brazil, most dieffenbachias like warmth (75°F) and mild nights but do not need sun to prosper. The plants need a loose porous soil, so add some chopped fir bark to the soil mix. Plants assimilate nutrients quickly, so be sure to repot every other year or feed on a routine schedule, that is, every other watering, except in winter.

Dieffenbachias are not the easiest plants to grow because they have an aversion to drafts and fluctuating temperatures. However, in an atrium or loft garden where ventilation is good, the plants are highly recommended. Here are a few species to try:

Dieffenbachia amoena. Broad leaves, handsomely variegated white.

D. bowmanni. Large leaves, chartreuse-mottled green foliage.

D. goldeiana. Bright green leaves; white blotches.

D. picta. Bright green leaves spotted white.

Other Plants

Here is a quick-reference chart of plants for skylight and loft gardens:

PLANT	DESCRIPTION	SHAPE	REMARKS
Acanthus mollis (Grecian urn plant)	Large deep green, lobed leaves: rigid flower spike	Rosette	Vertical accent
Aeonium arboreum	A handsome rosette of lush leaves to 3 feet	Rosette	For mass and horizontal accent; grows well in same pot for years
Agave americana variegata	Dark green and yellow leaves, highly sculptured; can grow to 5 feet across	Rosette	A dramatic display
A. attenuata	Gray-green foliage; twisted growth	Rosette	Fine specimen plant; needs little care
Araucaria excelsa	Needlelike, glossy green leaves	Pyramidal	Use as sculptural feature
Aucuba japonica	Polished dark green foliage	Dense leaves, round shape	For room corners
Begonia (angel wing)	Lush apple-green foliage; colorful pendant blooms	Generally a cascading plant	For color in hanging containers
Beloperone guttata (shrimp plant)	Small dark green leaves; colorful bracts	Sprawling	Old favorite
Camellia japonica	Dark green leathery leaves; large flowers	Irregular shape	Needs coolness at night
C. sansanqua	Dark green leathery leaves; small flowers	Irregular shape	Needs coolness at night
Caryota mitis (fishtail palm)	Wedge-shaped dark green fronds	Branching	Highly decorative
Chamaedorea erumpens (bamboo palm)	Erect canes with leaflets	Very vertical	Good in room corners; a stalwart grower
Chlorophytum elatum (spider plant)	A graceful plant with green arching leaves	A trailer when mature	Use on plant pedestals or in baskets

PLANT	DESCRIPTION	SHAPE	REMARKS
Cissus antarctica (kangaroo tree vine)	Scalloped dark green leaves	Upright or trailing	A good plant for shady places
Citrus (lemon, lime, orange)	Leathery, oval leaves; white blooms	Sculptural branching growth	Good floor plants for accent; need lots of water
Clerodendrum thompsoniae (bleeding heart glory-bower)	Bright green, large-leaved plant with stunning flowers	Low and round: dense	Accent plant for color
Clivia miniata (kaffir lily)	Straplike dark green leaves and orange blossoms	Low and lush	Reliable blooms; keep potbound
Coleus blumei	Many leaf colors	Dense and bushy	Highly decorative when mature
Crassula argentea (jade plant)	Small leathery leaves	Branching, full plant	Unusual and easy to grow
Cycas revoluta (sago palm)	Narrow dark green leaf segments	Vertical, delicate	Tough palm with good lines
Cymbidium devonianum	Grasslike foliage; delightful blooms	Upright, with pendant flower spikes	A touch of the exotic
Dieffenbachia amoena	Broad dark green leaves worked with narrow white stripes	Can grow to 6 feet	Good color: easy to grow
D. godseffiana	Yellow and green leaves	To 5 feet	Robust
Dion purpusii	Dark green leaflets	Arching and spreading	Excellent accent plant
Dizygotheca elegantissima (threadleaf false aralia)	Dark, shiny green, and toothed leaflets	Graceful and arching	A temperamental plant; grow it somewhat dry
Dracaena marginata	Spear-shaped dark green leaves	Branching, sculptural	A dramatic room accent against bare wall
D. fragrans massangeana (corn plant)	Tufts of apple-green leaves	Treelike when mature	Excellent vertical accent
D. werneckii	Striped leaves	Rosette tree	Stellar

PLANT	DESCRIPTION	SHAPE	REMARKS
Euphorbia splendens (crown of thorns)	Buttonlike dark green leaves; scarlet-red flowers	Branching and gnarled	Good pot plant
Ficus benjamina (weeping fig)	Leathery poplarlike leaves	Branching, graceful	Handsome tree
Grevillea robusta (silk oak)	Dark green fronds	Irregular shape	Different
Hedychium coronarium (white ginger lily)	Leafy plant with white flowers	Upright	Tough to bloom; needs heat and sun
Hibiscus	Large bright green leaves; huge flowers	Can grow to 5 feet; branching	A stunner in bloom and easy to grow; needs lots of water
Howea forsteriana	Dark green fronds	Drooping leaflets	Indestructible palm
Laurus nobilis (sweet bay)	Long, dark green, and leathery leaves	Compact, multi-stemmed tapering cone	Good in rows to guide traffic
Medinilla magnifica	Oval dark green leaves; showy pink flowers	Angled and long stemmed	Brilliant flowering plant; use mature ones
Monstera deliciosa (Swiss-cheese plant)	Mammoth, deeply scalloped leaves	Massive, sculptural	Always a good corner plant
Musa nana (dwarf banana)	Large dark green leaves	Upright	An oddity but nice
Nephrolepis exaltata bostoniensis (Boston fern; many varieties)	Cascading green fronds	Handsome rosettes	Splendid in baskets
Nerium oleander	Dark green leathery leaves; colorful flowers	Branching, spreading	Impossible to kill
Pandanus veitchii	Shiny green and white toothed leaves	Rosette; can grow to 6 feet in diameter	An overlooked fine display plant
Philodendron selloum	Deeply cut leaves	Branching, graceful	Makes nice accent

PLANT	DESCRIPTION	SHAPE	REMARKS
Phyllostachys (bamboo)	Grassy, needlelike leaves	Vertical, airy	Prettier than you think and easy to grow
Picea glauca Conica (dwarf white spruce)	Fine, soft, and bright green needles	Compact, pyramidal	Use where mass is needed
Polypodium aureum (hare's foot fern)	Large bright green fronds	Pendant	Excellent fern
Rhapis excelsa (lady palm)	Dark green fronds	Fan shape	Vertical accent
Schefflera acontifolia	Dark green leaves; frond growth	Canopy shape	Dramatic corner feature
Strelitzia reginae (bird-of-paradise)	Dark green leaves; striking orange flowers	Upright, to 5 feet	Nice for bloom; needs wet soil
Syagrus weddelliana (coconut palm)	Feather-leaved plant	Central trunk	Decorative; grows slowly

Artificial Light   Growing plants under artificial lights is a well-established hobby because plants thrive. Artificial light can aid plants in no-land gardens too, especially in loft and atrium gardens; use the standard bulb-shaped incandescent/fluorescent lamps to supplement natural light. (In hobby cart and shelf gardening, the fluorescent-tube lamp is used.)

Artificial light sources for plants have been greatly improved in the last few years. For example, there is a new incandescent growth lamp for plants that can be used in a standard porcelain socket. These lamps are specifically for one or two plants. There are also new indoor fixtures and floodlamps that make any loft greenery (even where there is little natural light) flourish. A standard incandescent 150-watt lamp placed in a ceiling fixture in the loft or atrium can help keep plants growing for years. For a 5 x 10-foot indoor garden, two 150-watt lamps will furnish sufficient light for most plants.

Fixtures for standard incandescent lamps or those for plant growth vary, but generally they are bullet- or canopy-shaped reflectors that direct light to the plants. These lamps add accent light as well as supply most of the beneficial rays needed by plants. The bullet fixture is handsome and blends with most interiors; the reflector hides the bare bulb from view. Track lighting hardware on which you place fixtures and lamps is available at suppliers and can be installed on ceilings; track lights are handsome and quite appropriate for any room. Contemporary fixtures can be angled to any direction. The movable light system known as Power Trac (by Halo Lighting Company) and Life Span (by Lightolier Company) can be used

ATRIUM GARDEN WITH LIGHTS

Design: Adrián Martínez

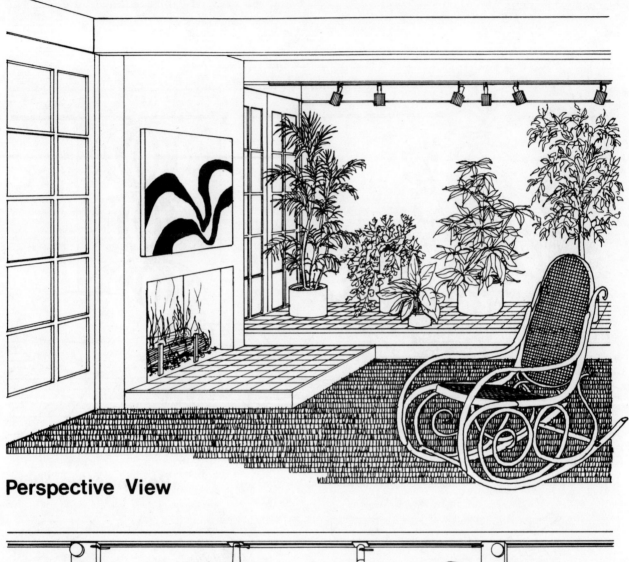

Perspective View

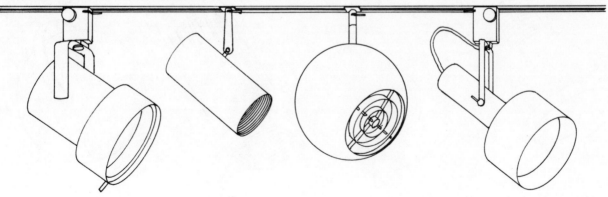

Ceiling Track Spot Lights

CORNER GARDEN WITH LIGHTS

Design Adrían Martínez

Perspective View

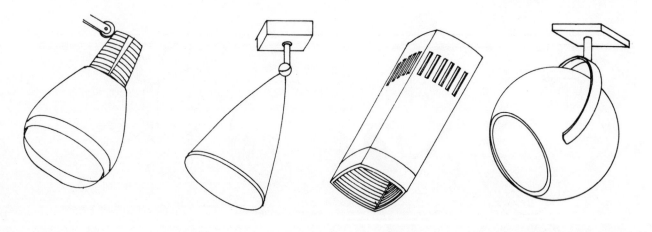

Mercury Vapor Floodlights

in straight lines or in an infinite array of patterns to cover almost any desired plant area (including windows).

New incandescent floodlamps specially intended for plant growth are now available. Manufacturers say these lamps have a better red-to-blue ratio than standard lamps. Mercury vapor lamps embody both fluorescent and incandescent elements in the same housing. There are several types of mercury vapor lamps: the easiest to use is the self-ballasting type called Fluomeric, manufactured by Duro-Test Corporation. Other manufacturers also sell mercury vapor lamps under various trade names.

No matter which lamp you use, be sure it is directed at the plant and at a distance of at least 36 inches from the top of the foliage. Installation should include a separate circuit to enable you to use the lamps alone because they must be on 12 to 14 hours a day to supply the necessary light source for plants.

Whichever lamps you use, remember that none are miracle workers by themselves. Plants still need water, humidity, ventilation, feeding, and pest control. Some of the lamps may be better than others for plant growth, but plants will grow and prosper under any light if there is enough illumination and sufficient day length.

7. Greenhouse and Patio Gardens

Both greenhouse and patio gardens utilize small outdoor areas, and you may have room for both. The attached greenhouse (a lean-to) is the most popular. It can be a commercially made unit or one you make yourself (less expensive). In either case you will need a foundation (concrete slabs or piers) for the greenhouse, and it is best to hire this construction out. Generally, a professional mason will be able to do this project for a reasonable fee. Look in the yellow pages of your phone book for help.

If you want a patio garden, partially enclose it with latticework or screens for an outdoor-room look. Embellish the scene with lovely hanging plants and some trees and shrubs in tubs.

Greenhouse Plants

There was a time when the term conservatory or greenhouse plants meant plants that had to be grown in controlled or special conditions. These were usually tropical plants. Actually, you can grow almost any kind of plant in a greenhouse: house plants do beautifully, but so do some small outdoor shrubs and even small trees. You can also use your greenhouse (and many people do) to start plants from cuttings or seed to save money.

Years ago there was a distinction between a warm greenhouse and a cool one. This misconception has been cleared up; we know that most plants respond just fine in a greenhouse where temperatures are quite like that of the average home. There is really very little mumbo jumbo to growing plants in a greenhouse, so forget everything you have heard about special equipment and so forth. All you need is good ventilation and some heating; the rest takes care of itself.

You can make your greenhouse a working one, that is, a hobby-type place where you putter and experiment with plants, or it can be a display place where you select and grow only a few dozen choice plants like begonias, orchids, or whatever you fancy. The greenhouse is truly an excellent no-land garden that offers a great deal of pleasure all year.

GREENHOUSES

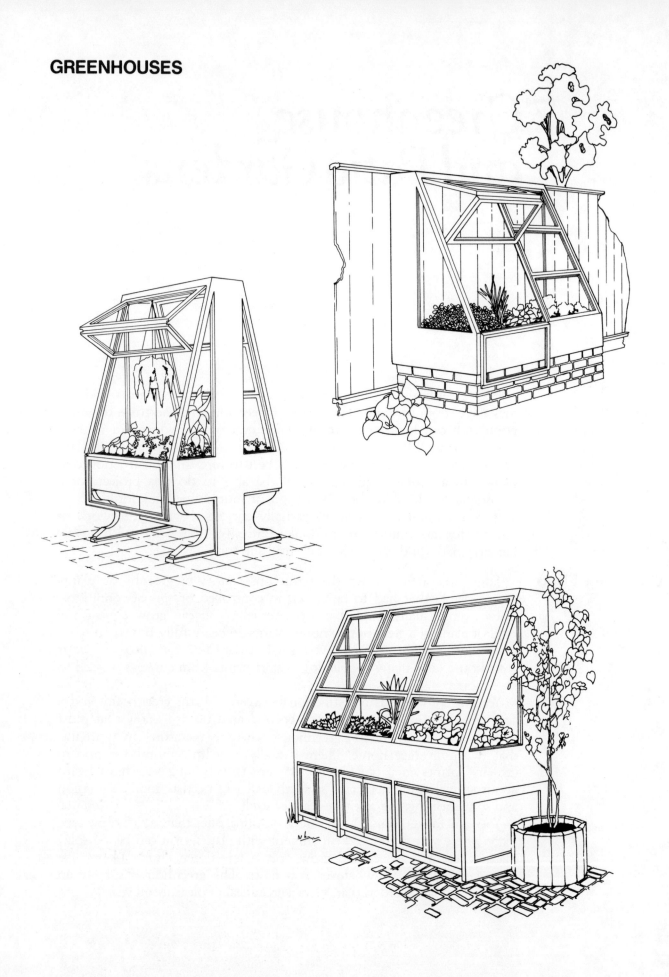

Greenhouse Conditions   There are no secrets to greenhouse growing, but you should know something about humidity, temperature, ventilation, shading, and heating.

Humidity   Average humidity of 30 to 50 percent is fine for most plants. High humidity can, when coupled with dark days, create a breeding ground for plant fungus and bacteria. Use a hygrometer to measure the moisture in the air. Remember that the more artificial heat you use in winter, the more moisture in the air will be necessary. On very hot days keep the humidity somewhat high, but lower it at night.

Many plants growing together create their own humidity, so expensive misters and foggers are not necessary unless it is very hot. Just water routinely; there will be enough humidity in a room of plants to create good growth.

Temperature   Maintain daytime temperatures of 70 to 80°F; night temperatures of 55 to 65°F. In winter you will have to adjust heat for very cold nights (and a few very cold nights will not harm plants). Sudden changes in temperature will harm plants. But if you carefully manipulate windows and

A small lean-to greenhouse is adjacent to a library and uses slat shelves to hold pots of plants. This area is totally charming and a good hobby greenhouse for the amateur gardener. (Photo by Clark Photo/Graphic.)

A typical commercial lean-to greenhouse design; the structure takes up little space, about 8 feet across, and can house dozens of plants. (Photo courtesy Lord & Burnham.)

doors, you can gradually cool summer evening temperatures. On very hot days, when doors and windows are open, inside temperature can pass 100°F, which desiccates plants and causes them to lose moisture fast. Spray and mist plants with water to keep them cool, and do provide shading (covered in a later section).

In winter it is much better to keep plants cool than too hot; they can recover from a chill but rarely from dehydration. On very windy and cold days, the temperature in a greenhouse can drop fast, so provide sufficient heat.

Ventilation   I consider ventilation more important than humidity or temperature because plants must have a good circulation of air. Good ventilation provides relief from the sun, helps control disease problems, and ensures good humidity. Plants do not object to coolness; indeed, they grow better in coolness as long as there is adequate ventilation.

Keep the atmosphere in the greenhouse buoyant and fresh, never stagnant or stale. Keep ventilation at a maximum. And even in winter be sure some air is entering the greenhouse. Hot air rises, so have some windows or vents at the top of the greenhouse. When windows or vents are open, warm air flows out, cooling the greenhouse and providing fresh air for plants.

Off the living room, this greenhouse is a lovely addition, bright and cheerful with many plants. It is a handsome garden. Space needed: approximately 4 x 8 feet! (Photo by Molly Adams.)

Shading   Direct summer sun can heat up a greenhouse and destroy plants. For example, some plants die overnight if they are subject to even one day of extreme heat above 100°F. And leaf temperatures over 120°F immediately scorch and kill plant cells. In most parts of the country, unless your greenhouse is at an east exposure, you must provide some shading for the greenhouse.

Use movable aluminum- or wood-slatted venetian blinds or bamboo rollups. Or try some nice curtains that break the sunlight yet allow some light through. Also excellent shading devices are special window trellage. Trellises (see Chapter 9) will provide almost perfect light for plants because they create alternating shade and light.

Heating   Greenhouse heating depends on where you live, the size of the greenhouse, and the design. Installation and operation of the heating unit is not too difficult, but determining what kind of heating fuel to use—gas, oil, or electricity—can be tricky.

Before you select a heating system, check local gas and electric rates. Decide which will be the most economical, and then investigate specific systems.

The gas-fired warm-air heater has a safety pilot and thermostatic controls. You may have to provide masonry or metal chimneys so fumes are released outside. A nonvented heater does not need an outlet chimney; the combustion chamber is sealed and outside the greenhouse. The heater extends about 10 inches inside the greenhouse and needs only a 17 x 20-inch wall opening. Both types of heater are approved by the American Gas Association (AGA) and are available through greenhouse dealers.

The oil-fired warm-air heater is small, able to fit under a greenhouse bench. It will furnish sufficient heat for most average-sized greenhouses. It has a gun-type burner, a blower, a two-stage fuel pump, and full controls. This heater requires a masonry chimney or a metal smokestack above the roof.

Electric heaters are also satisfactory for small greenhouses. These units are automatic, built with a circulating fan, but heavy-duty electrical lines are necessary. The heater and thermostats should be installed by a professional in accordance with local electric codes.

Saving Heat   A concrete floor is a remarkable heat storer; it absorbs enough heat during the day if the structure faces south to keep the room warm most of the night, even in very cold climates. Masonry walls opposite the glass wall will also absorb the sun's heat and store it for nighttime radiation. A wooden wall painted a dark color also helps to save on heating.

Thermopane, the insulating glass, can save as much as 30 percent heat in the greenhouse. It is however, more expensive than standard glass, so you might consider installing it only on the roof, where heat loss is greatest.

Another effective way of cutting down on heating bills is to install heavy drapes; they thwart cold drafts and keep the greenhouse quite

A splendid patio garden made beautiful by the dramatic trelliswork. All kinds of plants can be grown in such an area, and the garden is always inviting. (Photo by Max Eckert; Bernhard, Designer.)

A wickerwork structure dominates this patio area amidst a lush collection of leafy tropicals; a very charming picture. (Photo by Gamma Photo.)

warm at night. Weatherstripping will further keep cold air out and warm air in the greenhouse. Weatherstripping can cut heat loss by about 10 percent.

Patio Areas   In the 1960s, 30 percent of all new homes were built with what contractors called a patio—usually an 8 x 8-foot concrete slab in the rear of the home. This concrete slab is by no means a patio (a place to retreat to and enjoy nature) until some plants are in place. Also, a patio needs definition because an expanse of horizontal concrete, even with plants, is hardly pleasing. Basically, the no-land garden called a patio needs some type of vertical structure—a barrier, partition, or screening—to make it what most people seek; an outdoor living area.

Putting the necessary structures in place to create the patio atmosphere is not difficult, but it is not easy either. If you are handy, you can make your own screenwork, trellis fences, or other simple structures. More complicated structures like gazebos or enclosures really require some help from a professional.

Whether you build your patio yourself or have it done, make some rough sketches on paper before you decide on an overall plan. Just block out forms and lines; a precision drawing is not necessary. The lines and forms you put on paper will tell you a great deal; often an L-shaped enclosure, a canopy, or a simple divider is all that is needed to create the desired scene.

Once you have the basic plan and building finished, you will still need containers for the patio. Any of the planters described in Chapter 2 will work well for a patio. An average patio of 8 x 10 feet requires at least three or four long planters at the perimeter to frame the area and several large tubs to furnish mass and decoration. Use decorative pottery and urns and tubs; you want to create an attractive, pleasing setting while using very little land area.

Posts or rafters are excellent for hanging baskets of colorful flowering plants. On a patio you want many plants but not so many that you have a jungle you cannot penetrate; you want some open area for furniture and moving.

Patio Plants   The same kind of plants used in rooftop gardening are fine for the patio, namely, small trees and shrubs, annuals, and perennials. If you have room, espalier a few fruit trees for a handsome look. There are several midget vegetables called patio varieties for tub growing, but there is a limit to the kinds of vegetable you can grow on the patio. However, cherry tomatoes and lettuce in hanging containers will thrive. Be very careful about trying to turn the patio area into a vegetable garden because it will not have the character you are looking for. The patio is really a decorative or ornamental garden, not a farm.

On my small patio I grow annuals and perennials and a silk oak tree in a large box balanced on the other end of the area with a bougainvillea vine. The third corner has a group of rhapiolepis shrubs. Thus there are plants at three levels, which gives the patio a well-proportioned look.

PATIO GARDEN   Plan & Elevation

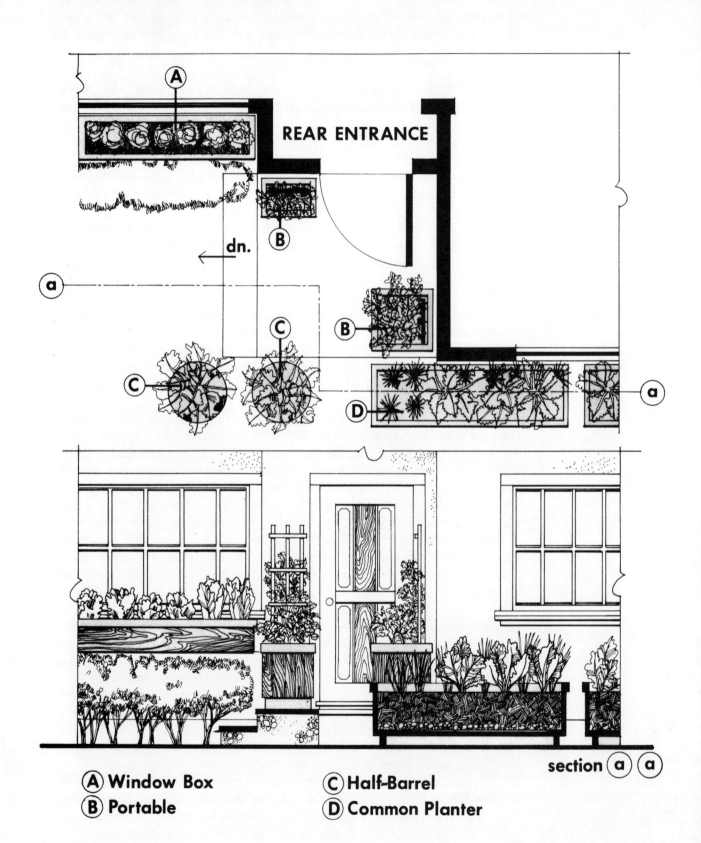

REAR ENTRANCE

A Window Box
B Portable
C Half-Barrel
D Common Planter

section a a

The house wall will serve as one vertical wall. To create balance, install a grid-type trellis at a right angle to the house wall. This type of patio is easy to construct and easy to garden in.

Patios are really for individual use, so just what you decide on depends on your own personal tastes. The point is that this type of no-land garden can be a valuable asset to the home and certainly a pleasure for daily living.

8. Insect and Disease Problems

Insects   Your indoor window gardens may be attacked occasionally by aphids, mealybugs, and red spiders. Outdoors, these insects plus scale, thrips, snails, and slugs may chomp on your plants. You must observe both indoor and outdoor plants carefully; you want to stop major infestations from destroying your gardens.

Eliminate insects by using either old-fashioned remedies or chemical pesticides. The old-fashioned ways are more time-consuming, but at least you do not have to have poisons in the area. Whichever remedies you use, know what bugs you are fighting.

Aphids   A plant infested by tiny aphids (plant lice) exhibits certain symptoms: it may lose vigor and become stunted, and leaves may curl or pucker as juices are drained out by the bugs. Aphids also carry mosaic and other virus diseases, so you *must* get rid of them.

An aphid is a small, pear-shaped, soft-bodied insect with a beak that has four needlelike stylets. These daggers pierce plant tissue and suck out plant sap. Aphids also secrete honeydew or sugar; this secretion is a great breeding ground for the growth of a black fungus known as sooty mold. Aphids are black, red, green, pink, yellow, lavender, or gray; young aphids may differ in color from adults.

Mealybugs   Mealybugs are cottony accumulations in the leaf axils or on leaf veins. These insects have soft, segmented, cottony bodies. Young mealybugs are oval-shaped, light yellow, six-legged, crawling insects with smooth bodies. They have beaks they insert into plant parts to get sap; as the sap leaves your plant, it wilts. Once they start feeding, the youngsters develop the typical cottony, waxy covering. They move slower and slower day by day, but they do not really stop moving, although you may not be able to discern this. Like aphids, mealybugs produce a copious honeydew that forms a breeding ground for sooty mold fungi and attracts ants.

Red Spider Mites   These tiny oval creatures are yellow, green, red, or brown. They have long legs and are almost impossible to see on a plant, but they do spin webs, which often give them away.

The two-spotted mite is the worst plant offender. Mites injure plants by piercing the leaves and sucking out liquid content from the cells. Foliage turns pale and may become stippled around the injured parts. If the infestation goes untreated, the leaves become rust-red and die. The plants may become covered with silken webs that the mites make as they move from area to area.

Scale   Scale are tiny and oval but noticeable insects with an armored shell or scales covering their bodies. Once settled on a plant, scale (mainly the wingless females) insert their mouth parts through a leaf and start taking in sap. They stay in the same spot throughout their lives, molting twice and laying eggs, in many cases giving birth to live young. The males have an elongated body and eventually develop wings, thus resembling gnats. Scale may attack leaves, although they are fond of stems. Plants with scale insects show damage on leaves as well as stems.

Of all the insects mentioned, scale is the easiest to combat because they are so easily recognized.

Thrips   Thrips are very small, slender, chewing insects with two pairs of long narrow wings. Their mouths are fitted with "tools" that enable them to pierce or rasp leaves. Adults are generally dark-colored and active between spring or summer. Some thrips are carnivorous and attack other thrips, and if the good ones overwhelm the bad ones, you can just sit back and watch the battle. Unfortunately, the bad ones usually win. Some thrips are active flyers, others just sort of jump around, and still others do not move much at all. Thrips leave a silver sheen on the foliage.

Chemical Preventives   Because there are so many insecticides and fungicides, and so many trade names for these products, you must know something about them to avoid confusion and possibly killing your plants with chemicals.

Chemicals to kill bugs come in many forms. Some are water-soluble; spray them on plants with special sprayers (always a bother). Powders or dusts are too hazardous and too much trouble to use indoors. Systemics are perhaps the easiest form of chemicals to apply. Systemics—insecticides applied to the soil—are very convenient to use. They come in granule form; spread the granules on the soil, and then thoroughly water the soil. The insecticide is drawn up through the roots into the sap stream, making it toxic. Thus, when sucking and chewing insects start dining on the plant, they are poisoned. Systemics protect plants from most, but not all, sucking and chewing pests for 6 to 8 weeks, so they need be applied only three or four times a year to protect plants.

How to Use Chemicals   No matter what poison you use, follow the directions on the package to the letter. In most cases repeated doses will be necessary to fully eliminate insects. Also, keep poisons out of reach of children and pets.

This closeup photo shows aphids, a common plant insect both indoors and outdoors. Although they appear large in this photo, aphids are about $^1/_{32}$ inch long.(Photo by USDA.)

For a good, general chemical that does not have an accumulative effect, use Malathion. If that does not work and you want to use other poisons, always follow these six rules:

1. *Never use a chemical on a bone-dry plant.*
2. *Never spray plants in direct sun.*
3. *Use sprays at the proper distance marked on the package.*
4. *Try to douse insects if they are in sight.*
5. *Do not use chemicals on ferns.*
6. *Always use chemicals in well-ventilated areas; outdoors is good.*

Mealybugs are another plant pest and seem to proliferate overnight; small attacks are easily eradicated, but large infestations can kill a plant. (Photo by USDA.)

Here is a list of chemicals, uses, and remarks about them:

TRADE OR BRAND NAME	PRINCIPAL USES	REMARKS
Malathion	Aphids, mites, scale	Broad-spectrum insecticide fairly nontoxic to human beings and animals
Diazinon	Aphids, mites, scale	Good, but more toxic than Malathion
Sevin	General insect control	Available in powder or dusts
Isotox	Effective on most but not all insects	Systemic; toxic but effective
Meta-Systox	Effective on most but not all insects	Systemic; toxic but effective
Black Leaf 40	Aphids and sucking insects	Tobacco extract; relatively toxic but safe for plants
Pyrethrum	Aphids, flies, household pests	Botanical insecticide; generally safe
Rotenone	Aphids, flies, household pests	Used in combination with Pyrethrum
Aerosol bombs	Generally sold under different trade names as indoor plant sprays	Can harm leaves if sprayed too close; also can irritate lungs; do not use outdoor spray for indoor plants

Old-Fashioned Insect Remedies

If you do not want to use poisons, try my unorthodox but efficient ways of getting rid of insects:

Alcohol swabs: Use standard rubbing alcohol on cotton swabs and daub the insects with them. This eliminates mealybugs.

Laundry soap and water: Use 1 quart of water to a half bar of laundry soap (not detergent). This eliminates such insects as aphids and mealybugs.

Nicotine solution: I gather cigarette butts and remove the tobacco. I let the tobacco steep in a jar of water for several days. Then with a cotton swab I daub insects with the solution. Aphids and mealybugs dislike nicotine as much as people who do not smoke.

Water spray: The simple but efficient use of water can eliminate many insects and their eggs. Use a strong spray at the sink and direct it at leaf axils and under the leaves. This procedure must be repeated every other day for 2 weeks.

Boiling water: Pour boiling water on the soil to eliminate thrips. Sometimes this works, but sometimes it does not; I imagine it depends on the type of thrip you are fighting.

Plant Diseases   If plants are well cared for, they rarely develop diseases. But if they do, know what to do; you do not want a costly plant ruined by fungus or botrytis, and a little knowledge can help you save infected plants. Most diseases will be minor, but if left unchecked they can become major concerns.

Ailments that strike plants are manifested in visible symptoms, including spots, rot, and mildew. Many plant diseases may result in similar external symptoms, so it is important to identify the specific disease to ensure positive remedies.

Unfavorable growing conditions—too little or too much humidity, or too much feeding—can contribute to disease, but diseases are mainly caused by bacteria and fungi. Bacteria enter the plant through naturally minute wounds and small openings. Inside, they multiply and start to break down plant tissue. Animals, soil, insects, water, and dust carry bacteria that can attack plants. And if you have touched a diseased plant, you can carry it to healthy ones. Soft roots, leaf spots, wilts, and rots are some diseases caused by bacteria.

Fungi, like bacteria, enter a plant through a wound or a natural opening or by forcing their entrance directly through plant stems or leaves. Spores are carried by wind, water, insects, people, and equipment. Fungi multiply rapidly in shady, damp conditions rather than in hot, dry situations; moisture is essential in their reproduction. Fungi cause rusts, mildew, some leaf spot, and blights.

Fungicides   Fungicides are chemicals that kill or inhibit the growth of bacteria and fungi. They come in dust form, ready to use, or in wettable powder. There are also soluble forms that have to be mixed with water and sprayed. Here is a brief résumé of the many fungicides available:

Captan: An organic fungicide that is generally safe and effective for the control of many diseases.

Ferbam: A fungicide very effective against rusts.

Karanthane: Highly effective for many types of powdery mildew.

Sulfur: This is an old and inexpensive fungicide and still good; it controls many diseases.

Zineb: Used for many bacterial and fungus diseases.

Benomyl: A systemic used for many bacterial and fungus maladies.

As with all chemicals, use them as directed on the package and with extreme caution. Keep all containers out of reach of children and pets.

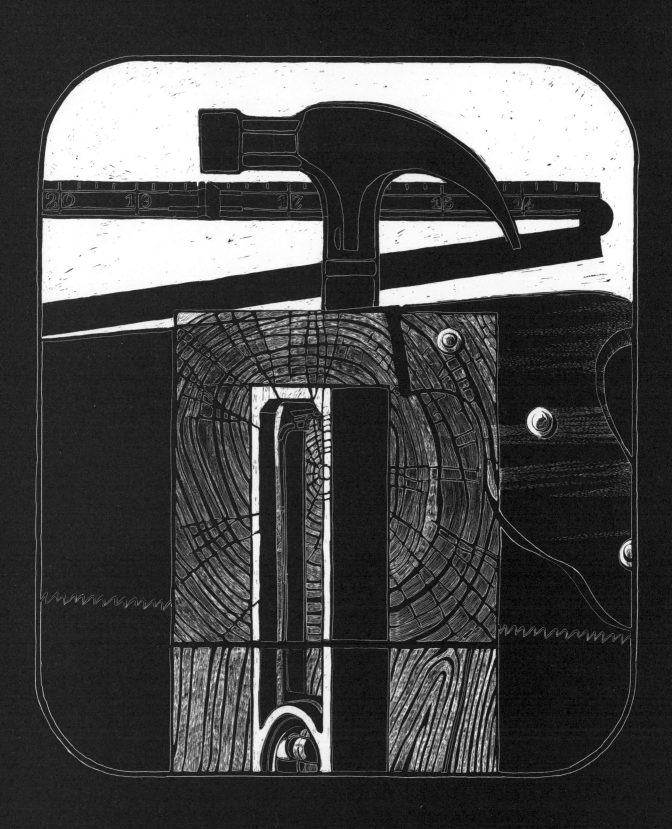

9. Materials and Construction

This book has many drawings of indoor and outdoor garden structures. Some are simple to build, others are far more complicated, but none are impossible or exorbitant in price. Some require little modification of existing construction, others require revamping an area, and some require only minor construction.

Do not let the idea of removing a window or installing a few boards and shelves stop you from having your garden. Of course, if you live in an apartment, you will be limited to shelf gardens and setups that do not destroy or mar the landlord's property. But sometimes, if you ask, you will be surprised at how flexible owners of buildings can be if you tell them how much it will enhance their property for you and for future tenants. (If after you do the job the owner raises the rent, do not blame me!)

Women and men both can wield a hammer with dexterity and build simple boxes and shelves. There is not that much physical prowess necessary, and your garden is a matter of the time and money you decide to put into it—and, of course, your personal taste. This is why so many different ideas are contained in this book; almost anyone can have a garden.

If construction alteration is necessary, do not pale at the idea. It takes about thirty minutes for a carpenter to remove existing window framing and another thirty minutes to install the basic framework. After that, do it yourself. It is not that hard, and the working drawings in this book should help considerably. (If you prefer, have the carpenter do the whole job.)

Do not be afraid to use skylights. They add light and are not that hard to install. Today, skylights are one-piece molded units that slip easily over headers (square boxes) in the ceiling. Once the opening is created (again, a carpenter can do this), you can install the skylight yourself. That is the way I did my recent garden room.

In other words, when there is some construction involved, such as removing a window or making an opening for a skylight, get some professional help. But to save money, do as much as you can yourself. Besides, there is a genuine satisfaction in making something yourself. Get in there and wield the hammer. It can be fun.

Wood   In Chapter 2 we talked only briefly about lumber. Here are some more tips and suggestions to help make purchasing and ordering of wood easy. Most lumber yards will, for a slight extra cost, cut lumber to a specific size, and this saves you the problem of, say, sawing a heavy 2 x 12 board. Lumber comes in standard lengths of even feet—6, 8, 10, and so on. Odd sizes have to be cut from even sizes, and you pay for the longer size and the cutting of the wood.

Woods are generally divided into two types: hardwood, such as oak, maple, and beech; and softwoods, such as cedar, redwood, and pine. Hardwood is tougher to work with and usually used for furniture or floors. Softwoods are easy to work with and for our purposes the best materials.

Wood is purchased by inches and feet. That is, a 1 x 2 x 12 board is 1 inch thick, 2 inches wide, and 12 feet long. These dimensions are not

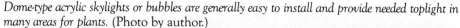

Dome-type acrylic skylights or bubbles are generally easy to install and provide needed toplight in many areas for plants. (Photo by author.)

exact, because in milling and sawing, some loss is created, so here is a chart to help you understand what actual sizes of wood you get:

Ordered Size	Unseasoned	Dry
2 x 3	1⁹⁄₁₆ x 2⁹⁄₁₆	1½ x 2½
2 x 4	1⁹⁄₁₆ x 3⁹⁄₁₆	1½ x 3½
2 x 6	1⁹⁄₁₆ x 5⅝	1½ x 5½
2 x 8	1⁹⁄₁₆ x 7½	1½ x 7¼
2 x 10	1⁹⁄₁₆ x 9½	1½ x 9¼
2 x 12	1⁹⁄₁₆ x 11½	1½ x 11¼

Unseasoned wood has not been dried or cured and is liable to more shrinkage.

Kiln-dried or seasoned lumber has a better surface and will not shrink.

There are various grades and kinds of lumber, which affects the price. For example:

Grades			Description
Redwood Clear	Red Cedar	Douglas Fir	
All heart	C and better finishes	C and better finishes	Top grade is expensive; used mostly for cabinetry
Select heart	C finishes	C finishes	Excellent for most uses; only slight defects
Construction heart	Merchant-able con-struction	Construction	Suitable for general con-struction; has some knots and defects; eco-nomical, but should be painted

Basically, side frames for windows will be 2 x 6 or 2 x 8 and shelves 1 x 6 or 2 x 6; these are the main dimensions you will be concerned with. For planter boxes, 2-inch stock is generally best. All indoor planter boxes should be made with seasoned lumber, but outdoor planters can be of construction heart. For outdoors, use redwood because it resists weather and needs no preservatives. Indoors, pine or fir painted the color of your choice works very well.

Glass   Glass is designated as SSB (single strength B grade) or DSB (double strength B grade). SSB is ¹⁄₁₆ inch thick and DSB is ⅛ inch thick. (The B designation does not mean that much as opposed to A quality.) You can also get glass in ³⁄₁₆- or ⁷⁄₃₂-inch thicknesses if more strength is needed. Like lumber, glass is sold on the even inch, so try to keep designs to even specifications to save money. It may not always be necessary, but it is a good idea to have glass edges finished, that is, smooth. Ask for ground edges or seamed edges.

Inserting glass in wood frames is not difficult if you have made the frames with a rabbet (notch) to accept the thickness of the glass. The glass should fit the wooden opening, with a tolerance of plus or minus ¹⁄₁₆ inch. Use a plastic-type glazing compound to install the glass in frames. These compounds come in pumpgun cans (you will need a can push); squeeze the compound along the perimeter of the frame; and then lay the glass against the compound and maneuver the glass in place. Scrape off excess compound with a putty knife, and then place small strips of wood (molding) on all four sides against the glass and glazing compound. Tack the small moldings in place to further ensure that the glass stays in place.

Shelving   Glass and acrylic are the basic building materials for plant shelves. Glass lets ample light enter a room, is relatively inexpensive, and always looks good. Acrylic is somewhat easier to cut than glass, is lightweight, and looks elegant. Acrylic sheet costs about 25 percent more than glass.

For glass plant shelves use ³⁄₁₆-inch-thick glass for spans to 30 inches; if the span is over 30 inches, use ⁷⁄₃₂-inch-thick glass for more durability. Edges on glass *must* be smooth; a glass dealer will have to do the smoothing. Always ask for a satin-smooth edge because it has more character than a simple seamed or ground edge. It takes a little time to cut glass properly, but it is not impossible. First practice with a glass cutter on scrap glass, or order glass already cut and processed at suppliers. (Professionally cut and processed glass will of course be more expensive than glass you cut yourself.)

When using acrylic, specify ¼-inch thickness; the edges of acrylic must be buffed to eliminate sharp edges. You can do the buffing at home, but it is better to have it done professionally. Use special acrylic tools to cut the materials.

Glass and Plastic Skylights   Glass skylights come in a range of shapes: single-pitched, double-pitched, hipped, gabled, hipped with ridge ventilators, and flat. The glass is usually glazed in metal, but wooden members can be used. Commercially made skylights are available, but generally you will have to have skylights made to size by sheet-metal houses to accommodate specific needs. As a rule, custom-made skylights are expensive, so if at all possible, use commercially made industrial factory skylights, which are cheaper. You can do your own glazing; just remember to use tempered or wire glass, to prevent accidents. (Exceptions are prefabricated greenhouses, which come with standard glass.) Many skylights leak, so glaze very carefully. Install glass on a caulking bed in the precast frame. Read instructions on caulking-compound packages carefully and follow them. If your glass is ¼-inch thick, a suitable ¼-inch groove must be part of the skylight members.

Installing a glass skylight frame is not easy because you must be precise. Leave an opening in the roof to accommodate the outside dimensions of the frame. Put in wooden headers and blocking, usually 2 x 4s but heavier if the skylight is large. Fit the skylight over this wooden frame, making sure it is flush so no air enters. It is important that your framing (blocks and header) be as absolutely square as the skylight. Apply mastic or caulking at the roof line, and put the skylight in place with screws.

Custom skylights—metal and glass units—are much more expensive than domes, but they impart a conservatory feeling to the space. You can use some handsome designs, but skylights are usually difficult to install and seem to frequently develop leaks. So unless you are absolutely set on the aesthetic quality of glass, give plastic domes first consideration.

The preformed or molded plastic skylight is a handsome addition and provides maximum light for plants. Acrylic plastic is available in several shapes and sizes; it is impervious to weather, lightweight, and easy to build with. Acrylic plastic skylights may be domed, right-angled, peaked, or triangular. The dome shape comes in standard sizes of 36 x 36, and 48 x 48 inches and so on. The other designs may not be in stock but can be ordered by your glass or plastic dealer.

The main consideration of any skylight or loft garden is to furnish natural light. The space chosen must have an area in the ceiling where one or two domes or skylights can be installed. Cutting out two areas in a roof is not that costly, and the domes are usually inexpensive.

The typical skylight garden can occupy the center of a room or be in a corner. All that is needed to define the area is a waterproof floor, usually of tile or brick. In any case, some professional construction may be necessary.

Trellises
Trellises—crossed pieces of wood—used as supports for climbing and vining plants are often overlooked in the gardening picture. Yet these old-fashioned supports, when used both outdoors and indoors, can transform useless space into cascading beauty of leafy plants. It is just thinking vertically rather than horizontally. Wood trellises are ideal indoors at the sides of windows where you want more space; they are equally good outdoors on rooftops and porch gardens in planter boxes for plants to climb on.

You can buy ready-made trellises, or make your own (actually very simple to do). Trellis is made from lath—thin ³⁄₁₆-inch-thick redwood or cedar strips about 1⅜ inches wide. Buy lath by the bundle from lumberyards. Install trellises with tacks or staples against inside window frames to provide additional growing space. The lath trellis is satisfactory, but for a more finished look, consider making the trellis out of 1 x 1 redwood or pine strips, maybe painting them to match the decor of the room. These wooden strips are more expensive than lathing but look better.

Trellis designs vary from grid to diamond to geometrical patterns. Some interior trellis-type dividers can be used as plant supports. These dividers are made of wood or wood-composition materials; the latter will not last long if much water gets on them, so shop carefully.

With trellises, a whole new world of gardening is available. Making and installing trelliswork is so simple that I highly recommend trellises for people who have little or no land to garden in.

Metal Bins   Galvanized metal liners for planters are not available commercially but can be made to size at sheet-metal shops. Remember to tell the craftsman that you want rolled edges and all corners seamed together to be water-tight. The bins then fit into appropriate wooden boxes. If you plant directly into the bin, remember to have a hole put in one end of the bin so water can drain out, and have the bin made so that the bottom slopes from 1 to 2 inches at one end so water can escape.

Galvanized liners are generally expensive. Less expensive are plastic flexible sheets. They are not as neat and do not look as good, but they do save money.

This last chapter (and the drawings throughout the book) are the basics that make the various gardens discussed work. There is a vast choice of gardens, and again, what you select depends on where you live, how you live, whether you live in an apartment or a home, and so forth. But no matter what the situation, if you want a garden—small, medium, or large—you can have one, and *without* any land.

This lovely patio area has become a trellis garden; it is easy to see how the trellis structure defines and creates the no-land garden. (Photo by Max Eckert.)